THE PERFECT TEN

TEN STUDENTS, TEN MINDSETS, ONE NEW
DEFINITION OF PERFECTION

DR. KEVIN LEICHTMAN

EduMatch Publishing

This book is dedicated to my wife, Anala, who relentlessly challenges every doubt I have about myself and encourages me to live up to my potential (and beyond) every day. I also dedicate this book to our sons, Asher and Arin, who blow me away with their perfectly unique traits and characteristics. I live in constant excitement and amazement of the way they grow into their own personalities. I hope they, like the incredible students in this book, continue to develop into their own selves unapologetically.

Lastly, I dedicate this book to the thousands of students who have touched my life and changed my perception of the perfect student. The ingenuity that all of you have shown me has made me a better teacher, and more importantly, a better man. May this book serve as a reminder that your voice and your experience can leave a positive mark on the world and on everybody you interact with, including your parents, your teachers, and most importantly, yourselves!

CONTENTS

INTRODUCTION

Hello, I am Dr. Kevin Leichtman, a former college failout. Not the introduction you were expecting? Good! I plan to take you on a trip outside of your comfort zone throughout this book as we explore the idea of the "perfect student."

I always had an idea of what the perfect student was. A bitter idea, because it was the opposite of me. I was a classic underachiever, barely graduating from high school. After a couple of mediocre years of work, I dropped out of my first college and transferred to my second, which I would fail out of in less than a year.

Throughout my academic journey, I wanted to be a perfect student. It just didn't fit me or feel right to even try. Deep down, I felt potential and a desire to be a success in school, but it couldn't seem to put that desire into practice. It was time for me to reflect. Maybe I got my definition of the perfect student wrong? The definition I imagined went something like this:

The perfect student has an unparalleled work ethic. They show up every day and complete all of their work on time, or even better yet, early. Note-taking is easy for them and they can obtain high scores on tests without even studying. Their grades are a point of pride and sound like the Fonz when he enters a room: "AAAAA." The perfect student makes sure to be involved in every sport and every club on campus. *They rack up wins in the yearbook superlative section and are loved by all. They never get in arguments with their friends or have any type of drama. An army of family and friends are constantly by their side, supporting their success and cheering for all of their numerous achievements. They have at least one full trophy case in their house.*

The more I allowed that definition to sink in, the more alienating it became for me. I couldn't live up to those ideals, so I moved rapidly away from them. After a largely negative experience with education, I was granted a third chance for a college degree at a small college -- on academic probation. I knew I would have to change my definition of perfect because there was no room for error. One low grade, and I would be gone.

Three years later, I received a bachelor's degree while celebrating my first time on the dean's list. I followed that success with a "perfect" 4.0 GPA throughout my master's degree. The final touches to my academic career included the completion of a Ph.D. program and publications to add to my name.

What was the difference? How did I go from a 2.0 high school student to a 4.0 graduate-level student? The classes were certainly more demanding and complex. My ability or potential didn't change. The answer begins with my definition of perfection.

I had to change what perfect meant. It was on me to shatter the view I created of the perfect student so I could create my own identity. The biggest thing missing from my definition was me! How could I be a perfect student if I built the model around other people?

My journey through education took years and thousands of failures, but a new idea of perfection led to a new mindset. I believed that I could live up to my potential and quickly found myself living above the potential I thought I had.

When my career shifted to education, I was given the opportunity to see a wide range of students. Some of them stood out, not because they were perfect students, but because they had created their own identity in academics. They had claimed their own version of perfect, and they lived it.

I also was given a front-row seat to a massive issue in education. Many of the teachers, administrators, and support staff seemed to have a similar view of the "perfect student" as I did a long time ago. I watched as students were overlooked by an education system that either didn't value the traits these wonderful kids possessed or didn't value the way those traits looked within these young men and women. Students who I felt were high performing and full of potential would be brought up in the teacher's lounge as "the bad kids to watch out for." I couldn't understand how these amazing contributors to my class could be such terrible students in the eyes of others. As I challenged them and reflected on their reasoning, I realized that the root of the problem rested in the idea of perfection. These young scholars did not look, sound, or act like the perfect students from the perspective of traditional educators stuck in an antiquated educational system. It became clear that advocating for my students would mean challenging expectations and helping educators to redefine the "perfect student."

This book features ten students. All of them were successful in school. All of them faced adversity from many sources. Each of them is incredibly unique. The common factor that brought them all to these pages is their phenomenal mindset. They each had certain traits and characteristics that stood out and carried them to success. Their potential expanded daily because of the self-motivation, drive, and determination they showed. To me, they were the perfect students.

Perfection

Let's be clear. We are here to break the stereotype of "perfection." Whether you are a student struggling to find your place in school, a parent wondering if your children are on the right track, or an educator who wants to bring out the best in your kids, it is time to confront and challenge the idea of perfect. This is your first step.

Write down your definition of the perfect student. Be as vivid and detailed as you possibly can be. What does the perfect student look like?

How do they act? What are their distinguishing characteristics? What is their personality like? Don't leave any stones unturned, and don't fall into the temptation of writing what you think you are supposed to write. Put in words whatever is on your mind!

I hereby give you permission to write in this book! If you think that writing in a book is not perfect student behavior, feel free to grab a post-it note and stick it in here.

My definition of the perfect student is:

Do you have a clear picture? Can you see the perfect student? Excellent! Now step two is to confront every aspect of what you wrote with honesty and a sincere desire to grow. Now, it is time to meet the Perfect Ten. As you read each chapter, make a note. Do these students fit your definition? Do their values match what you would expect?

These students have generously given us their stories and experiences so we can use them. Compare your (or your child's, or your students') journeys with theirs. Look at how they utilized their mindset to become their own version of a perfect student. Observe the success they brought about from their failures. Then, apply it!

Before I introduce you to my team of superheroes, it is necessary to dig deeper into the idea of perfection and how it relates to mindset. There are dangerous implications to a traditional sense of the perfect student.

1. SHATTERING THE PERFECT LENS

R esearch has shown time and time again how damaging perfectionism can be (Chang, Watkins, & Banks, 2004; Zannetti, 2013; Harari, Swider, Steed, & Breidenthal, 2018). Many do not realize how widespread the damage is. Some exhaust themselves by a drive to reach an unobtainable image of what "perfect" looks like in their head. Others, beaten by an insurmountable belief that they will never be perfect, grow to resent the characteristics they associate with perfection. Perfectionism adds to the expectations people have of themselves as well as how they view the expectations that others place on them. With no room for error, all fall short.

Perfection may hit hardest in grade school. Young men and women are encountering their own self-image and building the foundation of the mindset they will take with them to school and life. Surrounded by a box of their peers, it is nearly impossible to go through their daily life without comparing themselves to others. And what is that comparison based on? Typically, the lens of the parent, the teacher, the administrator, the school security officer, or any other adult in a power position. The "bad kids" are the ones that the adults identify as bad. The "perfect kids" are the ones that the school has determined to hold the best grades, achievements, and extracurricular awards. In other words, the adults create the scale of perfection by which all students measure themselves.

Narrative as a Mold-Breaker

Consider the mold of a perfect student. How are they portrayed? From my experience, the typical narrative in stories, movies, and television shows display mostly white students from mostly rural, upper-middle-class towns, wearing varsity letter jackets and smiling with perfect, shimmering white teeth. If the show features a character that does not fit that mold, it is usually to highlight their struggle in overcoming whatever obstacle kept them from being that perfect-looking student.

The stories we consume control the perceptions we have. If our narratives continue to be steeped in a singular view of perfection, we will miss the many routes to success that may be out-of-the-box or just different-looking from the common representations of success. What's more, we tend to push our expectations of perfect onto others. If you are a teacher, parent, coach, mentor, or even an older sibling, you are likely to take your idea of perfect and place it onto the people in your charge. A one size fits all narrative of success cannot cut it.

This book was written with the intention of disrupting the prevailing views of what a perfect student is. The ten students chosen for this book would not meet the typical portrayal of perfect. They come from a variety of backgrounds and experiences, with a wide array of goals and ideals. Success meant different things to each of them, and the path to all of their achievements was littered with doubt from traditional adults who felt that they did not match up to how a student should act. The shared experiences of these ten brave students were courageously given to help us question everything we know about perfection.

The voices of my perfect ten students have traditionally been left out in favor of the more media-friendly caricatures of the top students. Yet all of their stories are amazing tales of empowerment. They come from all walks of life and represent a variety of races, religions, nationalities, economic statuses, and other identifying characteristics. Each of them found a unique way to persevere, creating an individual story worth sharing. The uniqueness I saw in each of them was attributed to their mindset.

Mindset as a Lens to View Perfection

Mindset made the difference for these ten students, as it has for many of my students. Everything was different about these students, from their goals to their life circumstances to the opportunities available to them. Yet all of them became overachievers and rose above whatever expectations were placed on them. For each, they had mastered an element of their mindset and leveraged it to enhance their success inside and outside of the classroom.

Too often, mindset is an underrated factor when considering a student's approach to school. It is more likely to hear about grades, test performances, and attendance rates than it is to hear about the confidence, motivation, or resilience that a student shows. If the adults of a school are setting the tone for how students measure their perfection, mindset goes missing from the list. Schools fall victim to making the non-important things important and allowing the most important, foundational-building pieces to be forgotten.

It is time to bring mindset to the forefront of the conversations surrounding perfection and what it means to be a good student. Every student featured in this book displayed an impressive mindset that created openings for their success. While they were all well-rounded in many ways, each student will highlight one aspect of their mindset that stood out. This was done to show a narrative of empowerment and how each of these aspects of mindset can change the course of a person's life.

What's the Matter?

Teachers, parents, community leaders, mentors, students, and many others play a role in the development of each individual's identity. The way we identify a perfect student, the way we view mindset, the skills and abilities we prioritize as most important, matter. Your definition of perfection will influence those who look up to you, as well as yourself. There is an incredible price on the line of ignoring narratives that stand out or sound different. That price comes at the cost of identity.

Throughout the world, many students have the capability to contribute something amazing to the world. Yet, many of them do not reach their full potential. A large contributor to that is how they were described and understood by people they looked up to. If their greatest strength did not matter to their teachers, parents, or role models, then they may have given up that strength to focus on things that mattered more to someone else. When they compare their lives to their peers, they may glorify the behaviors and actions of others at the cost of downplaying their own abilities. This loss of identity can strike to the very core and hold anyone back from their full capacity.

The solution to lost identity is an infusion of narrative. It is vital for students to be able to see people who are similar to them in some way in a positive, successful light. We all want to be able to picture ourselves as a winner. Narratives of people who have already done it can help younger students to go get it done in their own, unique, perfect way.

Putting it in Context

If you are an educator, this book is meant to open your eyes to what you may be missing when considering your students' strengths and weaknesses. Allow your perceptions to be challenged. Confront the ideas that pop into your head as you consider some of these students who had low GPA's and barely made it to graduation. Could you shift your mind to include them in your definition of the perfect student? Can their mindset and the challenges they overcame convince you of a new standard of student? Will you honestly consider the harm that may be caused by the definition of perfection you portray for and enforce in your students?

If you are a parent, this book is meant to help you consider your priorities. Are you emphasizing certain results, or encouraging a mindset that your child will need as they grow and enter college or the workforce? How often do you talk about wanting to see A's and B's on a report card, versus how often you talk about the process of enjoying and engaging in the opportunities to learn more and be involved in school? And more importantly, what are you doing to foster your child's strengths as they seek and understand their identity?

If you are a student, this book is my promise to you that you can be exceptional. Soak in these success stories from ten students who were overlooked, undervalued, and left out of many conversations. Watch how they overcame anything that stood in the path they walked. Observe the way they utilized their mindset to prove anyone wrong who doubted them. Begin to locate yourself within these stories. What will your success story sound like? I cannot wait for you to build it and share it with the world. There is nothing more important than your voice. Allow these students to have a positive impact on you so that you can bring your voice to the forefront and have a positive impact on your friends, family, school, and community. I believe in you!

2. LEARN HOW TO HUSTLE WITH RAKHEE

" Everything you do today determines your tomorrow."

— RAHKEE

H-eartfelt
U-nderstanding that
S-uccess
T-akes
L-asting
E-ffort

———

Hustle is a difficult-to-measure quality. Yet, most of us know it when we see it. Hustle is that extraordinary ability that allows people to push past their limits. It is the drive from deep within that makes a person go the extra mile without being asked or told. Hustle is a vital piece of the Perfect Ten. For one often overlooked student, it allowed her to create a vision and speak it into existence. No matter the challenge, hustle became the foundation of her success.

Meet Rakhee

Rakhee, or Rah for short, defines hustle every day. She founded 5o9am.com (@5.o9am on Instagram), where she produces her own art and fashion design. Her unique style features beautiful, custom hand-painted artwork, typically on a variety of clothing items. Her artistic style has become massively popular at a rapid pace. A high achiever, Rakhee has created a powerful influence and a positive impact very quickly, starting her brand directly after finishing high school.

Before the success of her brand, however, Rakhee was considered an "at-risk" student. Several red flags existed in the system that showed her as a danger to not graduate. For many, they saw the data on her spotty attendance, numerous tardies, and courses not passed. Looking at the numbers caused them to overlook who she was, a determined young woman with the hustle to overcome any barrier.

Beating the Numbers

Rakhee's road to success was paved with doubters, naysayers, and a variety of setbacks. At a young age, she began elementary school while her parents were finalizing a divorce. This would send her and her two siblings to live with her father. While her academic ability was clear, she often struggled in school. Her head was in the clouds, drawing and designing in her sketchbook. When she was focused, her work was often overshadowed by her attendance record.

She was not alone in the struggle to make it through high school unscathed. She watched on as some of her friends transferred to alternative schools or left high school altogether. Other friends began to turn away from her and add gossip as fuel to the fire that was blocking her success. Every twist and turn led to more adversity.

Rakhee had always expected to graduate and make a success out of her high school career, but the numbers did not match the success she had hoped for. Entering her last year of high school, there was very little room for error. She explained,

A lot of obstacles stood in my way during high school, a lot of people didn't like me for their own personal petty reasons so that put me in a lot of conflict and drama throughout the years, keeping a decent GPA in order to graduate, while also juggling a part-time job that was literally right after the last bell of the day. Believe it or not, the most difficult thing about high school for me was getting there on time.

None of these issues were separate. They were a swirling vortex, weighing on her mind as she constantly went from school to job to home to help her family. Her grades slipped further behind as her work life became more hectic. She did not even have an easy route to get to school, having to rely on friends and family members for rides.

The odds were stacked against Rakhee. The further along she went in high school, the farther away her goals seemed to be. With the potential of not graduating sinking in, she had every excuse to quit. That is exactly the moment when her hustle kicked into a gear that I had never seen in my students before. Perhaps this quote from her best explains how she was able to find success:

"The only person who is stopping you is you." And that quote is relevant to almost every situation in life because only you have control over your own future & life whether you want to stay stagnant or progress is entirely up to you."

Hustling for Passion

Hustle is a trait of passion. It is not a characteristic that one wakes up with or automatically has. It is fueled by a passionate desire to achieve greatness and go beyond the expectations of the many to accomplish the results of few. People who hustle harder have a powerful reason for waking up in the morning. They know what they want out of life and are willing to whatever is necessary to even have a chance of making their dream a reality. That was the secret to Rakhee's success.

While many of her peers were nonchalant and undetermined about their future, Rakhee had a focused mission to take her artistic talent to another level. She explained, "What I truly wanted to do was art & fashion; it pushed me to want to succeed and finish school so I can ONLY have time for the things I wanted to occupy my time with." Her passion became the driving force for her success. As life and school became more difficult, her motivation only became more clear. She had to succeed to earn the ability to put her time and energy where she wanted to put it.

Rakhee's senior year was not perfect. Friends continued to move into and out of her life as their priorities caused them to drift away from her. Teachers continued to doubt her ability and judge her heavily on her absence and tardy marks. Work after school presented multiple challenges. However, those issues were minor in the face of the major goals she had set for herself.

Furthermore, having a vision allowed Rakhee to use high school for the skills she needed to survive in business. She stated,

School taught me a few things that I still use in my everyday life, like discipline and when I say that I don't mean the teacher hitting you with

a ruler I mean self-discipline, putting my school and homework before any other activities I had planned. It also taught me how to be efficient with time, getting the work done before the deadline. Both self-discipline and time efficiency work hand in hand when running a business.

Whenever people doubted her (which I saw often), they would quickly realize their mistake. Rakhee's self-discipline was incredible. With no apologies and no excuses, she would ensure that she was ten steps ahead of everybody else. She never worried about her situation and only focused on the potential she had and the elements within her control.

Entering Rakhee Into the Perfect Ten

I always enjoyed Rakhee's impact as a student. She would ask intriguing questions and show a perspective that many would not consider, including me. She was not afraid to be a leader and stand out in class. While her effort was always striking, it was not the reason why I picked her for the Perfect Ten. It was because of a much more subtle but powerful moment.

On a slow day in class, I asked her about her dreams and passions. As if she had rehearsed the moment in her head, she pulled out her sketchbook. A variety of patterns, symbols, and clothing styles filled each page with care and dedication. She did not tell me that she *wanted* to be a fashion designer. She told me that she *would* be a fashion designer. It was clear to see that this was not a passing trend, but a mission that she had undertaken with the full capacity of her heart.

We had many conversations following that day, which allowed me to see her progress in decision-making. Rakhee did not have a clear route to success, and she didn't have a long list of mentors in the fashion industry to help her get started. What she had was a sense of hustle. By trial, error, and a complete lack of fear, 5o9am.com was launched. She took her future into her own hands and brought her vision to life from the ground up. Through self-discipline, a strong sense of responsibility, and a willingness to outwork anyone and everyone, she is now climbing the ranks of the art and fashion community while leaving a hugely positive influence on her following. She continues to advocate for teens and young adults by letting them in on her journey, placing herself as a role model to many.

Rakhee became a part of my new definition of the perfect student. Seeing her name on at-risk lists made it clear to me that a perfect student does not have to have perfect grades or attendance. If I never asked her a question, I would have no idea why she missed class so often or what struggles she faced on the path to her diploma.

So what does the perfect student have? Passion! A student who has an unstoppable, unquenchable desire to achieve anything in life can surmount the loftiest obstacles in pursuit of it. Rah is my proof that a strong hustle can take a student to new heights.

My New Definition of the Perfect Student

The perfect student:

- **Hustles harder than their peers because of an unyielding passion that they possess.**

Your New Definition of the Perfect Student

Did this chapter impact your definition of a perfect student? How important does the characteristic of hustle rank when considering the strengths of a student? Flip back to the introduction and look over your first definition. Reflect on what you said and what you read. Is your definition firm, or is it shifting? Write down your reflections in this space, or begin revising your definition:

Mindset Lesson—Hustle Harder

A true hustler knows how to leverage their intrinsic motivations. It is pretty common to hear "hustle" in terms of business, like having a side hustle, for instance. Yet attaching extrinsic motivations like money to hustle actually makes that trait weaker. A key to increasing your ability to hustle is to learn what your intrinsic motivations are. Do you want more control over your life? Do you want to have a stronger pursuit of your passions? Do you want to open up a career field or opportunity for yourself? Whatever makes you tick at the deepest levels is what needs to come out to the surface for you to hustle harder.

Rakhee was able to tap into her intrinsic motivation to increase her hustle. Her method is as follows:

What motivates me to keep hustling isn't the money or any materialistic object, it is simply to live life on my own terms so that means I have to bust my butt every day to achieve that goal in order to make it into my reality. Before I set my mind on something and go along with it I ask God for guidance & protection over my project then the rest is up to me to stick with it and fulfill my goals & duties I set for myself.

To increase your ability to hustle, try these steps:

1. Define your passion and make what you want clear
2. Declare your passion to the world (your family, your friends, your faith, or anyone important to you)
3. Write down the responsibilities and duties you will have to keep to succeed
4. Have a clear vision of what this success means to you
5. Put into words how hard you are willing to work to bring this success to reality

Overlooking the Hustler

How do people like Rakhee remain under the radar? Students who hustle and put in extra work should stand out. This desirable quality goes unnoticed quite often, unfortunately. Hustlers are constantly working, thinking, dreaming, and acting on their dreams. This can lead to a lack of focus in the present as they constantly map out their future.

For Rakhee, many teachers assumed the worst of her. They did not see the quality of a hard-working hustler with big dreams. They saw a talkative girl who was off task. They would not hone in on her conversations, assuming that her talking in class was typical high school gossip. They did not realize that she was planning out her vision, testing marketing strategies, and bouncing branding ideas off of her friends.

Because Rakhee's hustle often went unnoticed, teachers were not able to tap into her potential and see how creative and driven she actually was. She is certainly not the only student like this. A metric ton of overlooked talent walks schools across the world because hustle does not always look studious and methodical. Students with hustle are out-of-the-box thinkers with an entrepreneurial spirit. Do not miss the hustling student by confusing them with a distracted, chatty teenager. Listen to their goals and watch their brainstorming shift into world-changing actions.

Make it Yours

What are your passions? What are your hobbies? Where do you like to spend your time most? Many of us have answers ready at a moment's notice for these questions. If you don't have an answer ready, this may be your call to get outside of your comfort zone and engage more with life. Finding your passions is a key step to finding your purpose.

However, if you do have answers ready to those questions, it's time to take it to another level. Are you making the most of your passions? Are you committed to turning your passion into your life's work? Are you outworking the people around you? Are you outworking people around the world who you might not be able to see?

You can't hustle at half speed. If you want to keep up with changemakers like Rakhee, you will need to go full-throttle at every turn. Analyze your vision, be clear about what you are seeking, and then go get it!

3. LEARN HOW TO BE YOURSELF WITH DOMINICK

"If you're not a bully, you're doing something right. You can very easily make fun of someone. A negative input for a negative output. If you can resist that, you are a good person."

— DOMINICK

B-old
E-nvisioning of

Y-our
O-wn
U-tility

———

B
e yourself. It's one of the first pieces of advice you hear in grade school. It also happens to be the least encouraged quality in the average school. Being yourself requires people to be open to everything that makes them unique and helps them to stand out among others. Unfortunately, most school activities are designed to show students how to fit in and be like-minded. Classroom policies, rules, clubs and extracurricular activities, dress codes, and a variety of other norms exist in preventing students from creating and embracing their identity.

Meet Dominick

Dominick happily describes himself as belonging to nerd culture. He said,

I've been enveloped in it since I was four years old. I was shown all the star wars movies and from there it never left me. Star Wars 'forced' me into the abyss that is fandom. From that came superheroes and comic books and that fueled inspiration for art and they all worked together.

His eclectic taste in art, movies, comic books, and other forms of media has led him on a wild adventure into his own identity.

At one point in his school career, Dominick would have met all of the traits of a typical "perfect" student. He was timely, studious, and high-achieving. He took pride in his work, and it showed through every project or assignment he turned in. Yet a piece of him always seemed to be missing. It was a quiet, subtle part of him that crept into every aspect of his life. Slowly, his work became more sporadic. His attendance followed suit as he racked up more and more absences. The "perfect" student that Dominick used to be had faded into a quiet, reserved fragment of his potential.

An Identity Stolen

High school brought out the best in Dominick, but not through the path that was expected. He learned by unlearning and confronting the issues that held him back. It took many failures and moments of frustration to bring those issues to light. This started with his willingness to be in school. He explained to me, "I would find excuses to be home or go home. I just didn't want to be there. That was the number 1 thing. I would miss assignments, especially during sophomore year."

It was easy to see why Dominick wouldn't want to be in school. He was antagonized and bullied on a regular basis. People noticed how passionate he was for superheroes, comic book characters, sci-fi movies, and the art he was producing. It brought negative and persistent attention to him. While the bullying did not reach physical extremes, it wreaked havoc on the identity and culture that Dominick was trying to develop.

The bullying was effective in challenging Dominick's identity. He always had the desire to speak up, defend himself, and embrace his interests, but those desires failed him in the moments where he needed it most. He described, "when you're being antagonized, it all leaves you. Every form of, I'm going to say this… You're hearing what they're saying, and it clouds your thoughts and what you want to say." That cloud began to consume him in a mission to hide and avoid those situations. This meant hiding from school, dodging classes, and lowering his self-expectations as well. He did not do this happily, but he allowed himself to become a person that he did not want to be.

An Identity Retrieved

Three difficult years of high school left Dominick with very little outside of the label of "nerd" and a report card that showed only a shell of his capabilities. Entering his senior year, a different person emerged. The real, authentic Dominick showed up at the start of the year. He was brimming with confidence, full of pride, and clear-minded about his hobbies, passions, interests, and goals. This young man was ready to take on the world!

It was not a new identity that emerged. It was the real him. Dominick had finally learned to accept that what he was passionate about would not appeal to everyone else. That didn't matter anymore, because he knew it was important to him. He said,

I didn't bend the knee to anyone who told me not to like those things. That's the important thing is to not give up. Who is anyone to tell you what to like? I'm so glad I didn't listen to them. This stuff is cool!

Where in the past he would be at a loss for words, he began to embrace the words that he needed to say all along: that he likes who he is.

Dominick's story of bullying started and stopped with his perspective on his own passions. When he let bullies invalidate his experiences, he was an easy target to give up his definition of self. When he controlled his own identity and weighed the reasons behind his passions over the irresponsible words of people who didn't have his best interest at heart, he was able to embrace his identity and fully live out his potential. He expounded on that realization:

If your heart is really in something and you feel that drive and motivation to do it, forget what everyone else says. You've already made up your mind. You don't need the validation of any other person. Think back on what they made fun of you for. What good did this passion bring? Is that more powerful than the insult? I think so. If you really love something, you should recognize that as a tool to just forget about what anyone else has to say about it.

At his core, Dominick knew that his interests went beyond the idea of being a nerd. He liked things like Star Wars because of the family bonds it created. He reflected, "Sitting in the theater with my grandfather. Nobody can take that away from me no matter how many names I'm called. It makes the people that say that irrelevant." His joys and passions had a purpose. As they brought his family closer, it also engaged his curiosity for the arts. An accomplished young artist, he would not have explored that talent without the motivation from the comic books and graphic novels he enjoyed.

Through his adventure with bullying and missed classes, all the way to an accomplished high school graduate ready to take on the world, Dominick became himself. He rejected everyone else's definition of him and placed his identity on his own shoulders. Armed with passion, purpose, and an unrelenting desire to take charge of his life, he learned how to be himself.

Entering Dominick Into the Perfect Ten

The more that Dominick moved away from the typical definition of the "perfect student," the more impressive he became to me. He would not have found his identity so strongly if he didn't face bullies and confront the impact they had on him. His struggles in school forced him to carve out his own path.

As a teacher, I saw many students who were isolated or left out. Cliques would form and absorb people into a shared identity. Often, students would lose themselves to the person that others wanted them to be. Dominick chose a different path. He experienced all of the pains of not fitting in. Instead of changing himself to suit others, he used those pains as fuel to advocate for students like him who felt left out and excluded.

Seeing a need for an inclusive environment in school, Dominick stepped out of his comfort zone to create an official school club for people interested in comic books, superheroes, and similar interests. As the student leader of this club, he brought together many students who had felt isolated and gave them a space to feel empowered and understood. His reasoning was, "There's a decent amount of kids in my spot in high school; they feel like they don't have a place where they can go and talk to people." Confident in his own character, he dedicated a large portion of his senior year to build that confidence in younger students.

Dominick was always a great student and a joy to have in my classroom. I enjoyed all of the artwork he shared with me and the many conversations we had about movies we liked. He even spent extra time teaching me about the Marvel and DC universes and helped me understand the differences. Those qualities made him a fantastic student, but that's not what made him a Perfect Ten student.

Simply by being himself, Dominick stood out as a memorable student worthy of the title of "perfect." He struggled with his identity, the self-described "nerd culture" that made him the center of attention for bullies. He overcame that struggle and came out of it as a better version of himself. He embraced his passions and used them to become more social and engaging. Instead of fearing bullies, he began talking to people from all social groups without fear of standing out or being different; different was now a point of pride. He would never walk into the room and blend in again.

My New Definition of the Perfect Student

The perfect student:

- Hustles harder than their peers because of an unyielding passion that they possess.
- **Embraces their identity, honoring and valuing the unique qualities and passions that they possess.**

Your New Definition of the Perfect Student

Did this chapter impact your definition of a perfect student? How important does the characteristic of being yourself rank when considering the strengths of a student? Flip back to the introduction and look over your first definition. Reflect on what you said and what you read. Is your definition firm, or is it shifting? Write down your reflections in this space, or continue revising your definition:

Mindset Lesson

Surely you have heard the advice, "be yourself." I always remember the classic line from Robin Williams when playing the Genie in Aladdin. He turns into a bee to tell Aladdin to "bee yourself." It seems like the most simple advice, but applying it can be incredibly difficult.

How can you be more intentional in finding yourself and being true to who you are? Dominick gave this pointed advice:

Find ways to laugh and smile. Don't try to pursue things that you know aren't you. If you are hanging out with a group of kids, watch for moments when you look at them or hear what they are saying and you're like man, this is not me, this is not who I am.

He noticed that each time he tried to fit in, he found himself jumping more out of his own character. He learned how to be himself by drawing barriers, protecting his identity, and refusing to change that identity for anyone else's benefit.

Here are five steps to help you be yourself:

1. Know your passions and be very intentional in engaging in them
2. Value your passions, hobbies, and interests above the perceptions that others have of you
3. Embrace your identity - it will take away the power anyone has to make fun of it
4. Help others to gain confidence and explore their passions
5. If the school environment isn't conducive to your learning, safety, and comfort, advocate for yourself and change it

Overlooking the Individual

People like Dominick do not always get the opportunity to express who they are. In a highly structured school, uniformity and discipline can interrupt the identity creation that all students are going through. Regardless of the identity that is being built, the key to the matter is why that identity is being built. Without providing opportunities for students to explore that why, schools do not allow students to live up to their full potential.

It was eye-opening to understand why Dominick felt so strongly about nerd culture. I quickly learned that it was not about the games, comics, or movies, as much as it was about the strong bonds he created with his family. He may not have realized that without deep introspective reflection, either.

Whenever you notice someone who seems quirky or different from you, it is important to understand why. What do their quirks say about what you consider to be regular? What about their identity differs from yours? Asking these types of questions will help you understand and get to know others better, while also helping you dive into your own individuality and understand it.

Make it Yours

There are two important realizations that anyone must make to truly be themselves. First, realize that the world is much bigger than you or your current surroundings. Second, realize that this giant world needs your unique contributions, and only you can fill your shoes.

Dominick learned it best during the tragic school shooting at Marjory Stoneman Douglas High School. Attending the neighboring school, he participated in a student march. He explained, "when we were going out to march, it made me want to do more. It fed into my responsibility feeling. Like Spock said, 'The needs of the many outweigh the needs of the few.'" Through that devastating event, he learned the importance of being himself. He couldn't help the community or be a positive impact on anyone if he couldn't first see and believe the positive in himself.

What do you have to offer the world? What individual traits do you bring to the table? Reflect on the things you find most important in life. Consider your passions and your joys. What would those things look like if you put your whole heart into them without fear or apology?

Stepping into your identity forces you to step away from the control of others. Peer pressure, bullying, and always trying to fit in will lose their grip on you when you build a strong knowledge and understanding of yourself. Begin (or continue) that journey today so you can hold all of the power in your own life, and so you can use that power to empower others.

4. LEARN HOW TO BE MENTALLY TOUGH WITH HILARY

" School was like a workout, when your muscles are burning and you can't do it but you need the gain so you have to keep going. No matter how much weight/pressure you have to keep going. It is up to you!

— HILARY

T-enaciously
O-ptimistic
U-nder
G-rueling
H-eat

————

How tough are you? It is a question that is expected in a gym or a competition for a contact sport. It is not a typical question in a school building. Academics at all levels rarely talk about toughness. Yet, that is what is needed to excel in school. A certain degree of mental toughness is a prerequisite for success in school and life. I thought I knew exactly what mental toughness was until I met Hilary.

Meet Hilary

There is no mistaking the toughness that Hilary brought to the table. In the boxing gym, nobody could mistake her short, lightweight stature for weakness. Her vicious hooks, uppercuts, and power punches could stun a person twice her size. She brought that same toughness and determination to every task, whether it was working late shifts, studying hard in school, or writing her own novel.

Hilary had all of the tools and abilities to meet the standard definition of the "perfect student." She read books. Outside of school. On purpose! She loved to read, write, and come up with unique ways to express herself. Add a strong work ethic and a thick layer of toughness, and most would say she had everything it would take to be a top-level student. Those thoughts were betrayed by the reality: that she might fail out of high school.

Tough by Force

Toughness was a trait that Hilary always had, but did not always have to use. Born to a close-knit Mexican family, she had plenty of love and support from her parents and siblings. Her parents worked especially hard to ensure Hilary could live comfortably, yet they also taught her often to embody their work ethic. She explained, "I was a princess... A spoiled brat. But I also knew nothing would be handed to me that I didn't earn. I had to find a balance between those two things."

While school was a safe haven at a young age, middle school hit Hilary harder than her expertly thrown boxing punches. Friends would betray her and try to get back in her good graces as if it were a routine. She often found herself as the focal point of rumors, gossip, and bullying. It was common to see her walking the hallways alone, avoiding the crowds and the drama that would follow.

Trust became a double-edged sword. Hilary did her best to make friends and socialize. When someone would take advantage of her kindness, she would shrug her shoulders and try again. Her optimism was tried and tested repeatedly. Unfortunately, that relentless trust and admiration for her friends would lead her down the most difficult path she could have walked through her academic career.

Bottoming Out

High school provided many of the same challenges for Hilary, yet it lacked much of the support and guidance that middle school had offered. While Hilary drowned in the drama, her grades went completely underwater with her. She said, "I didn't prioritize myself. I put others ahead of me and put their futures above my own." It was normal to see her helping friends with their homework, which meant she ran out of time to do her own.

Freshman year left Hilary with the reality that she might not be able to graduate. Holding a GPA near 0.0, hope seemed to be lost. She had incredible talent as a student, but her kind heart and inability to pull away from the pressure of her social life led to a disappointing year. She had bottomed out.

The Toughness Test

Facing a breaking point, choices had to be made. Hilary began to apply what she had been learning at the boxing gym and what she had been reading in the courageous characters of stories she enjoyed. It was time for her to leverage her toughness and fight for herself! She stated, "I had certain people I was scared to let down. People that always believed in me. Fear over disappointing someone – myself and the people that always believed in me." In the same way that she would get in trouble for caring too much about what her peers thought, she started to consider what her friends, family, and trusted mentors would think if she became a success. It was time to rise to the potential that so many saw in her.

A new young woman seemed to emerge from the pressure and heart-break of failing. Hilary made a decision to put all of the fight she had into her own success. She described the way she overcame her situation: "Self-love and self-respect are key. Being able to advocate for myself and being confident. I had to say that I am better than this (event, moment, outcome, etc.)." Just like she used to advocate for all of her friends, she began to advocate for herself.

The decision did not come without resistance. Hilary's life became more hectic throughout her high school years as she balanced full-time work with her struggling GPA. On top of that, she became involved in relationships that would require her attention and bring her around more people that needed her help. This was the test. The various responsibilities and challenges she faced would determine if she was truly ready to prioritize herself. Navigating her time and energy seemed impossible, yet she was unwilling to give slack in any aspect of her life. Could she balance it all?

Tough in Tears

The end of high school saw Hilary in tears often. I worried that the tough girl had reached her breaking point. On a near-daily basis, she would come to my room early for a quick cry at the beginning of class. With a silent stream of tears lining each cheek, she would assure me that she was fine. Her reassurances were grounded in her concept of toughness, which she described as:

Even if I had to work at 3 to stay afloat, even if I had all F's, working my butt off every single day to raise it, I knew myself. As long as I felt like I could do it, I'd be fine. I'd stress and cry but I knew I could do it. That helped me push to a 3.0 from almost 0.

Unlike other students I had seen, Hilary embraced the stress. Instead of fighting back tears and acting unbothered, she moved with vulnerability and genuine sincerity. She invited opportunities to feel overwhelmed. She explained, "It's okay to break down. You don't always have to be that tough person who has that demeanor. It's okay to take five minutes to break down." By inviting those moments in, she was able to confront and overcome every voice that said she could not do it.

Confidence fueled by her endless supply of mental toughness led Hilary to become an incredible success story. Many assumed she would drop out of school, giving her little chance to even finish her senior year. She overcame that doubt and graduated with a respectable GPA, all while maintaining her relationships, helping her family, and obtaining several promotions in her job. The many twists and turns that originally threw her off course became the exact path she needed to begin believing in herself.

Entering Hilary Into the Perfect Ten

I had a strong picture in my head of what mental toughness was. As an avid gym-goer and a wrestling coach, I saw toughness all the time. The look was the same, no matter who was sporting it. Toughness would come with an air of confidence, eyebrows set like stone in determination, chin puffed out, and eyes looking through their target. That kind of toughness belonged inside the gym. I felt that way until I met Hilary. Her version of mental toughness transcended location and worked within the classroom space.

She brought the mentality I had seen in athletes to the classroom. Like a bodybuilder struggling through a set of squats, she would sit at her desk struggling to meet the requirements of the many classes she needed to catch up on. When it got too tough, her tears would only signify the fact that she was going to try harder. The confident determination that set in her face was identical to Olympic gold medalists as she strived with every fiber of her being to reach her goal.

Hilary entered my classroom as a very good student: an avid reader and writer who had the potential to be a star. I believed in her potential and looked forward to her work. However, she did not become a "perfect" student from reading and writing often. Her perfection sprang from her imperfections, along with the toughness that it took to succeed in spite of those imperfections. She was willing to battle for every grade, each assignment, and all opportunities to become the best version of herself. That fight showed me an element of perfection that I had never seen in a classroom before.

My New Definition of the Perfect Student

The perfect student:

- Hustles harder than their peers because of an unyielding passion that they possess.
- Embraces their identity, honoring and valuing the unique qualities and passions that they possess.
- **Has an unyielding mental toughness that pushes them past any barrier or limitation that stands in their way.**

Your New Definition of the Perfect Student

Did this chapter impact your definition of a perfect student? How important does mental toughness rank when considering the strengths of a student? Flip back to the introduction and look over your first definition. Reflect on what you said and what you read. Is your definition firm, or is it shifting? Write down your reflections in this space, or continue revising your definition:

Mindset Lesson

Mental toughness, by nature, must be relentless. You need to bet on yourself in every situation and believe that you are capable of seeing it through. There is no room for doubt, negative self-talk, or apathy. It is an extreme mindset that, if embraced, can lead you through the most difficult tasks and challenges.

Hilary had two things to say about gaining mental toughness. She said, "You have to be able to do it alone, but it helps to have positive support and encouragement." Mental toughness starts with you. Your willingness to take all of the responsibilities of your future success and ignore all excuses that pull you away from that success is a requirement. When you have put the ownership on yourself, then it is important to seek advice and accountability from others. Hilary believed that it was much easier for her to remain tough and focused when drawing energy from people who supported her and wanted to see her succeed.

Following Hilary's lead, here are five steps you can take to improve your mental toughness.

1. Say daily affirmations of confidence (look up affirmations or create your own)
2. Write down your go-to excuses and reword them in a way that forces you to own up to them and be accountable
3. Communicate daily with people who encourage and inspire you
4. Exercise and push yourself physically to practice toughness from a different level
5. Welcome adversity as a necessary step in your path to greatness

Overlooking the Mentally Tough

Mental toughness can quickly become an assumption. Students like Hilary show that they can handle anything and overpower any situation that is not in their favor. Hilary had plenty of people who just assumed she would be fine because she was tough. This led to people using her to help them with work, taking advantage of her toughness, and assuming that she would never have an issue.

Mental toughness does not mean invisible, and it certainly doesn't mean invulnerable. The mentally tough people in your life do not exist to take on more or to have to deal with extra difficulties due to their strength. Instead of pushing them to their breaking point, see what happens when you build up mentally tough people. Encouraging them and working towards goals with them can be as empowering for you as it will be for them.

Make it Yours

Mental toughness does not have to come from negative situations. It certainly will not come from your comfort zone, however. Pushing your limits should become a consistent practice as you increase your toughness. Be warned that you will not be able to push your limits physically, mentally, or emotionally if you don't have a purpose behind doing it. This means that you should make your mental toughness very personal. Understand why you want to be tough and what you want to accomplish.

As you reflect on your mental toughness, consider your reasons for wanting to be mentally tough. What drives you to success? What makes you want to have a never-give-up attitude? Finally, consider the state that Hilary was in as a student who was written off by many. Seeing her succeed and crush her goals should tell you something about yourself… What can you accomplish if you put your full heart into it?

5. LEARN HOW TO BE OPTIMISTIC
   WITH CAMILO

Tough times were only as temporary as I made them. If I wanted to change where I was at or what I was dealing with, then I needed to make changes in my life. Every day is an opportunity to be great!"

— CAMILO

O-verwhelmingly
P-ositive
T-emperment
I-ndifferent of
M-isfortunes,
I-mpasses, or
S-imple
M-ishaps

———

Optimism is a vital skill to extreme success. It is nearly impossible to reach a result that you cannot imagine happening. When goals become challenging and insurmountable odds loom, the only hope for success is the ability to remain optimistic. This mindset skill is not limited to just "looking at the bright side of things." Optimism can become a character trait, symbolizing a confident belief in the potential of good coming from any situation, whether seemingly good or bad in the moment. For this student, optimism made the difference between accepting mediocrity and reaching for greatness.

Meet Camilo

From the eyes of my 5'6" frame, meeting Camilo was akin to standing in front of Andre the Giant. His demeanor fit the same description. Camilo was a towering presence, but his temperament was kind-hearted and calm. A smile was a permanent fixture on his face. He was loaded with potential in school, sports, and life.

Many were fooled by Camilo's positive attitude. Not because his persona was fake, but because it led them to believe that his life was perfect. How else could a guy be this happy? An outsider would believe that he never endured any form of stress or pressure. They didn't realize that Camilo's attitude was a choice. Had he dwelled in the negatives of his life, his path would look vastly different from where it took him. By choosing positivity and acting on it every day, he elevated himself to a level that very few believed he could reach.

Positive Through Pain

Camilo described his childhood as being a family-oriented, Hispanic, Catholic upbringing. He was brought to the United States by his parents as a mere one-year-old. They had planned the move to the States to provide their kids with a better education and more importantly, a better opportunity to succeed in life. Despite his parents' best efforts, this move would prove disastrous on his young childhood. He was constantly uprooted as his family moved from place to place. He and his sister often took care of each other while his father worked two jobs and his mother worked a full-time warehouse job. Then at times, his father became ill and unable to work, and even tougher times loomed. He explained,

I can remember the days where people from our church would come to visit my family and bring us food because we didn't have enough money for food. But one thing is for sure, my father never quit.

At a very young age, he understood that their life would not be easy. Nobody could hide the struggle that his family was in as they settled into a new life in a new country. To add to their challenges, his father was constantly ill and fearful about his health. Camilo said about the experience, "I learned life isn't all sunshine and rainbows. I didn't get to experience the joy that most kids had growing up. Rather, I was constantly on my toes prepared for the worst possible scenario." He had to prepare himself at a young age to step up and fill the responsibilities of his father if need be.

Still, Camilo found ways to remain positive about this tough childhood despite the odds. He was deeply involved in the Catholic church, where his dad took pride in taking him and his sister every Sunday. The pinnacle for his father at church was when his kids became altar servers, and he was able to see them worship. The emphasis on faith allowed Camilo an opportunity to bond with his father and learn from him as they worshipped together. He also looked back fondly on what his parents would sacrifice to give him a sense of normalcy. He said, "One thing I always appreciated about my parents is that every birthday they made it a mission to make sure we had a birthday party and invited our friends." These events would make daily difficulties much more manageable by providing a beacon to look forward to. Along with those happier moments, his family instilled in him the values of God, family, and education. This guiding philosophy helped him to stay focused, enduring throughout the many challenges he faced.

Joining the Team

While Camilo made it through a tough childhood relatively unscathed, he needed more to maximize his potential. He was a good student and a respectful young man, but he continued to look for an extra push. It would have been easy to settle for mediocrity. Nobody would have faulted him for having average grades and staying in the middle of his class. He knew that if he remained comfortable, he would sink.

Athletics became the push that Camilo would need to take his optimistic outlook to another level. Always a positive thinker, he was now faced with real obstacles in the form of other, very angry people, coming right at him. Similar to the circumstances of his childhood, he would have to find ways to stay calm, collected, and positive no matter how the situation felt like at the moment. One thing was for sure, Camilo didn't let people bully him or push him around. He held his own every day.

Camilo thrived under the spotlight of his football and wrestling career. He earned Coaches Player of the Year in the 2016 football season and earned numerous student-athlete academic awards in both football and wrestling. However, it wasn't the competitions that kept him going as much as it was the coaching. He explained, "A few of my coaches (more notably my football coach and wrestling coach) went from an athletic coach to a life coach, and as a young kid, that was probably the best thing for me. They helped me pursue life after college…" He had assembled a team of adults who cared for him, understood him, and pushed him to be his best. This network of support led him to greater than expected accomplishments.

The Bright Side of Responsibility

A sense of maturity surrounded Camilo at all times. I noticed it as soon as I began coaching him. He could laugh, joke, and smile with anyone, yet his mind was always set on a mission. It was a constant awareness of the bigger aspects of life that were yet to be fulfilled. That maturity led to him seeking out supportive coaches and mentors. He understood what it meant to be coachable. By listening to the advice from trusted mentors and drawing from his childhood experiences, he was able to make a very difficult decision: He willingly gave up on sports.

The conclusion was not easy, but it had everything to do with his future goals. He said, "I needed to make the unpopular decision to forgo collegiate athletics and continue my education at an accredited university." He could have played college football at a smaller level, but his big dream was to succeed in business and life. He chose to stay

in Florida and attend college far enough from his parents to give him a sense of independence, but close enough to get home fast when needed. This experience would help him cultivate a business mindset.

He knew that football would only distract him from his purpose at the collegiate level. Besides, he had already received what he needed out of sports: a never quit attitude. By utilizing the mindset he acquired from his past experiences, he was able to persevere and make the most of the opportunity. A recent college graduate, he has already stepped into an exciting salaried position!

Entering Camilo Into the Perfect Ten

Camilo was defined by his strong mind and strong body. He had many of the characteristics of a "perfect student." What stood out to me was how easily he could have slipped from that characterization. Most teachers did not know of his struggles. They didn't understand the responsibilities that burdened his young shoulders to ensure his family had food, money for rent, and everything else they needed to survive. His optimism was the mask that covered his reality.

The most impressive part of Camilo's character was the ability he had to find the help he needed. By seeking out coaches and their wisdom, by purposely applying optimism to his life, by actively working on his motivation, he carved his own path to happiness. His humility kept his optimism as one of the best-kept secrets in the classroom and on the field. The success story he created was done very quietly through adversity, but his optimism allowed it all to look easy.

A moment that defined his "perfection" for me was in the postseason wrestling tournament of his senior year. He had been on a losing streak he couldn't seem to shake. Close in every match, he kept coming up short. He was somehow able to advance through the district round, and he left his mark on me during a match in the

regional tournament. He faced elimination in what could be the final match of his career, down by a point with seconds remaining. With all of the determination and heart he could muster, he launched a desperation move and found a way on top of his opponent to win at the last second. After the adrenaline rush had faded, I asked him why he tried that move. He said his coach had taught him a new move during warmups, a move that, if performed wrong, would lead him to lose the match within a second. He then explained that he could only accept losing after exhausting all other options, but he couldn't end his career quietly. Always the optimist, he believed that in any situation, there was still a chance for him to win, no matter how bleak things may have looked.

My New Definition of the Perfect Student

The perfect student:

- Hustles harder than their peers because of an unyielding passion that they possess.
- Embraces their identity, honoring and valuing the unique qualities and passions that they possess.
- Has an unyielding mental toughness that pushes them past any barrier or limitation that stands in their way.

- **Knows how to remain optimistic and apply it to their everyday lives.**

Your New Definition of the Perfect Student

Did this chapter impact your definition of a perfect student? How important does optimism rank when considering the strengths of a student? Flip back to the introduction and look over your first definition. Reflect on what you said and what you read. Is your definition firm, or is it shifting? Write down your reflections in this space, or continue revising your definition:

Mindset Lesson

The first step to increasing optimism is to realize that it is not a fixed feeling. People are not born being either optimistic or pessimistic. This is a quality that can be changed and utilized for your advancement. Optimism also is not dependent on your life, experiences, or situations that you have faced. Take this trait into your own hands and leverage optimism to make the most out of your life.

Camilo believed that it was important to seek help and advice as you navigate the challenges of school. He added, "Every one of us has a fire inside of us; our job is to make sure we fuel that fire but not to the point where we let it burn us down. Always have confidence in yourself despite what anyone has to say about you." Through seeking mentorship and fueling your passions, he believed that any student could stay optimistic and on track to success.

Incorporating Camilo's advice, here are five steps to improve your optimism:

1. Keep a friend group full of positive thinkers
2. Find mentors and support from adults who are optimistic and believe in you
3. Join sports, clubs, or other activities that will force you to deal with adversity in a positive manner
4. Write in a gratitude journal daily
5. Create a vision board that portrays a positive future for you

Overlooking the Optimist

Not every smile comes with a hidden hardship behind it. However, it can be dangerous to assume that an optimist has it all together. Many confuse optimism for happiness because they come with similar characteristics: smiling, laughing, light-heartedness. It is important to note the difference, however.

An optimist has simply given awareness to the idea that the future can be better and brighter. Be aware that they might not be living in a better, brighter present, and their past may have come with even more challenges. Students who are optimistic may need encouragement, guidance, mentorship, and genuine friendship from people who are willing to understand what made them an optimist. Do not take their positive outlooks for granted and assume that their life is perfect. Instead, see how you can create a positive impact on them!

Make it Yours

Your current situation does not dictate your ability to think positively. Challenge yourself to practice gratitude. It is also important to realize that there is no downside to optimism. The worst thing that can happen to your optimism is that a situation doesn't play out as well as you hoped it would. However, remaining optimistic, you will begin to use those moments to plan how that let-down will lead to an even brighter future. Positive thinking breeds positivity in the same way that negative thinking breeds negativity.

Reflect on your standard emotional reaction to news, whether good or bad. Are you quick to spot the upside? Do you get down on yourself in advance when faced with a new opportunity? How often do you daydream about a bright future versus the amount of time you spend worrying about whatever is coming next? Every day will lead you closer to a new future. Whatever you envision is more likely to come to fruition. Will you allow your mind to lead you to the best possible outcome, or will you allow it to consume your thoughts with worst-case scenarios? Make your decision, then begin to practice!

6. LEARN HOW TO BE RESILIENT WITH HANNA

" Today when I try to understand all the bad decisions I took, I think I was always postponing the encounter with the person I really needed to be... the one I deep inside always knew I could be."

— HANNA

R-esponding to
E-very
S-ituation with
I-ntegrity,
L-iveliness, and
I-ntensity,
E-nvisioning the
N-ext
T-riumph

———

R esilience is on the shortlist of traits most people describe when discussing mindset. It begins with the understanding that life will not always go as expected. Failures, setbacks, and obstacles (whether avoidable or not) will push against everybody. The ability to push back, stand up, and keep going marks the resilient warrior. It is a vital skill because it can put a person's reactions to any situation in drive, whereas a lack of resilience can put their reactions in park on the side of the road. For Hanna, it may have done more than that. Resilience may have saved her life.

Meet Hanna

Hanna was a young woman of many talents. From a young age, she engaged with life and explored every opportunity she had to learn and grow. She was an imaginative reader and thinker, often daydreaming and letting her mind carry her away. She developed many passions which manifested into a well-rounded balance between athletics and academics. She can play a beautifully relaxing, melancholy tune on the piano, and then follow it up by heading to wrestling practice to take on the toughest athletes in the room. It was clear from a young age that Hanna had the ability to be a champion at anything she put her mind to.

Hanna's position in this story is unique. Unlike the rest of the Perfect Ten, Hanna did not attend a school where I taught. I was connected to her through a wrestling club where I helped coach. That connection proved to be one that would teach me much more than I was ever able to teach her. Hanna redefined the way I view resilience, and her story (and my view of resilience) is still being written in many ways.

Building the Foundation

Hanna grew up in a large, mixed-race Brazilian family surrounded with love and support. She often spent time with her grandparents, aunts, and uncles. This loving environment is what she attributed to her curious and happy nature. She explained, "I was always such an adventurous little girl who would be able to have fun with anything that was around me at the time." She formed many powerful relationships with friends and family as she began to develop her many passions and skills.

The loving family that raised Hanna was not free from struggle. However, they did all they could to protect her from the burdens they faced. She said, "I would never think that the times me and my family would spend days at my grandma's, was because of the unpaid bills." Her happiness and safety were made a priority, so she had no reason to fear or worry. Hanna's family also placed a strong emphasis on faith, which she also attributed to her positive outlook and joy for life.

The first major test in resilience would happen when at age 15, Hanna and her family relocated to the United States in search of better opportunities. She had practiced English in Brazil, but the language barrier and culture shock hit her quickly. She described, "the only thing that stood in the way of my success was myself. I was always too scared of trying, scared of what people would think about my accent, about the way I looked, or scared about not being good enough to read in front of the whole class." Those fears would block her initial attempts to succeed in school in the way she had in Brazil. Where she was once a top, multi-talented student, she began to struggle to stay above average. Nothing was easy anymore.

When it seemed as though Hanna was bound to crash, her resilience came into play. She pushed to master English and understand the culture, diving into everything that would help her succeed in the U.S.A. This included her participation in the wrestling team, which would give her practice with her athletic talent as well as with her communicating and networking. After a difficult first year, she began to overcome many of her initial fears. The language and culture became more commonplace for her, and the Hanna that her family had always known began to reemerge in their new location. Her outgoing nature and drive for success led her towards the top of the ranks in her academics and her wrestling career. She had passed the first test in resilience.

From the Summit to the Shadow

It may have seemed like Hanna had overcome her biggest obstacle in life, yet this calm brought with it the storm of the century. Many would say that moving to a new country and quickly finding success is an incredible sign of strength. However, as Hanna braced for bigger successes, life had a much different plan for her. She entered the final years of her high school career filled with high expectations, a world of potential, and plenty to lose.

Hanna placed a goal to win the wrestling state championships in her senior year. She entered the year a strong candidate to do just that, while also balancing competitive grades and an overall positive school performance. With much on the line, something gave from within her. She explained, "It was senior year, and I had received many offers for wrestling in college, yet I skipped way too many classes, my grades and performance decreased. I lost the scholarship and the opportunity I fought for three years to have." What began as a promising year for a scholar-athlete quickly became an ever-looming shadow that cast itself over her potential.

The disaster that brought this havoc into Hanna's life was a familiar figure to many teens. It was an issue of identity. She told me,

My happiness and emotional equilibrium were in a boy's hands, the fights with my parents were endless, my mom would cry because of me for days. And all I kept doing was hiding myself from the reality behind a large, dense, and obscure cloud of nicotine. My mind was so full of all those everyday momentary feelings, that my internal light started fading more and more. I put myself in a dark room and had no idea how to get out from there. I lost my identity. I did things that I would never think I was capable of. I became the worst version of myself. The idea of organizing the mess inside me was worthless, just so I was.

It was a subtle movement in her life that slowly took control of who she was. She had lost the discipline, the focus, and the boundaries she had created to ensure her success. As her identity faded, her opportunities began to vanish with it.

The Not-so-Happy Ending

High school did not end with an amazing comeback story for Hanna. Her wrestling career began to decline along with her school performance. She competed at the state wrestling tournament and fell short of the expectations that her coaches and parents had for her, and far shorter than her own expectations. A rare second chance was given to her to compete in another prestigious tournament, but she suffered an injury shortly beforehand. That inability to make a comeback only contributed to the spiral of lost identity and further questioning of her purpose.

Resilience Restored

Resilience can be a complicated trait because even if a person has it, it doesn't mean that they are always ready to use it. Hanna had resilience in bundles, yet she was having trouble bringing it to the surface. As her identity continued to slip, her desire to bounce back diminished. She had entered a survival mode, doing only what was necessary to continue moving forward. She credited the positive influence of her coaches and teachers like Mr. Carr, who poured extra time and energy into her to help her reach graduation.

Leaving high school, Hanna had to accept the end of her wrestling career and the beginning of very hard work. Her life was in a drastically different position than she had expected as a young girl. This was exactly what she needed to bring her resilience back to the front of her mind. She said, "I realized that it wasn't about wrestling. That I could find other passions and other things I also could be good at and even be recognized for!"

As quickly as the shadow came into her life that clouded her judgment, light washed over her and brought out her spirit better than before. She began to fight for her passions furiously. She refused to accept an identity that did not belong to her any longer. Through faith in God, reliance on her family, and a determination to live out her potential, she began to restore her character. Her life was marked with long and late shifts at work, followed by early mornings at a small school to begin her college journey. She did this with no complaint or fear, welcoming every opportunity to come back to herself.

Hanna's story of resilience continues into the present. Resilience is the ability to bounce back, and she decided to bounce back in every way possible: physically, emotionally, mentally, and spiritually. She recovered from her old wrestling injuries and prepared her body for success. With a recovered GPA at the college level and a renewed effort in every aspect of her life, Hanna will be heading to a new university to restart her wrestling career and continue her college academics!

Entering Hanna Into the Perfect Ten

Resilience is the ultimate equalizer when facing any problem or challenge in life. Hanna is proof that it doesn't matter how quickly a person figures their life out, as long as they have the resolve to bounce back from failures and mistakes. She went through the most difficult route she could have faced for her journey, yet that road was paved with the experiences that she would need to develop into the woman she wanted to become.

I related to Hanna's story in many ways. What stood out to me was not the way she recovered from her lost identity or how she showed resilience. It was the honesty and genuine appreciation she had for the process she had gone through. She understood that while not ideal, every mistake she made was a vital step in becoming a resilient, capable adult. The important step in resilience is not *when* a person starts. It is the fact *that* they start. Hanna found her way back by forgiving herself for her

mistakes, learning from her failures, and refusing to let her positive characteristics be silenced.

My New Definition of the Perfect Student

The perfect student:

- Hustles harder than their peers because of an unyielding
  passion that they possess.
- Embraces their identity, honoring and valuing the unique
  qualities and passions that they possess.
- Has an unyielding mental toughness that pushes them past any
  barrier or limitation that stands in their way.
- Knows how to remain optimistic and apply it to their everyday
  lives.
- **Is committed to bouncing back and remaining resilient,
  no matter what happens to them.**

Your New Definition of the Perfect Student

Did this chapter impact your definition of a perfect student? How important does resilience rank when considering the strengths of a student? Where in your life have you faced a situation like Hannah's, and how did you find new hope? Flip back to the introduction and look over your first definition. Reflect on what you said and what you read. Is your definition firm, or is it shifting? Write down your reflections in this space, or continue revising your definition:

Mindset Lesson

A vast majority of books and resources on mindset will mention the importance of resilience. I often see the perspective that resilience is on a scale, where you either have an abundance of it or too little of it. However, the real importance of resilience is in your ability to apply it. However much resilience you believe yourself to have, it does not matter if you aren't able to utilize it in a time of need. Hanna discovered that when she let her initial mistakes lead to bigger mistakes, without attempting to bounce back. Once she applied her resilience, it changed her circumstances drastically.

Hanna gave advice for how to improve resilience. She said, "Allow yourself to make mistakes, but do not let them define who you are! Learn from them, have self-love and nothing in this world can harm you." The idea of self-love is not to give yourself an excuse for slipping out of character. It is about giving yourself the forgiveness needed to move past those moments of identity loss so you can be resilient and recover as quickly as possible. Here are five steps to improve your resilience:

1. Write down aspects of your character that are important to you and non-negotiable
2. Find role models and mentors who embody the traits you want to have
3. Practice forgiving yourself for small mistakes
4. Be future-minded by reflecting on what your next positive step forward is, instead of dwelling on what negative steps happened in the past
5. Ask for help and gather support before you need it

Overlooking the Resilient

Resilient people like Hanna are often met with fear. Instead of celebrating the bounce back, many want to avoid hearing about the fall. Most of us tend to seek out happy stories without honoring the difficulties that preceded the happy story. I was very lucky to not overlook

Hanna. By sharing her struggles, hardships, and mistakes, I was able to learn so much from her!

The resilient students that you meet deserve to have their stories and experiences honored. Do not shy away from the tough moments that made them who they are. This doesn't mean you should harp on those experiences or force someone to rehash their worst moments. To truly understand the resilient student, give them space and your attention so they may share their experience. Allow them to take the lead and determine what was important about their journey.

Make it Yours

Tragedies and setbacks do not necessarily increase your resilience. Rather, they reveal the resilience you have already built. You do not have to feel like a large mistake is necessary to learn how to become resilient. No matter what your life situation is right now, you can build your resiliency and prepare yourself for moments when you'll need to use it.

Make resilience a trait you can rely on by first having a very clear snapshot of who you are and who you want to be. The more clarity you have on that picture, the easier it will be to spot when you are off track. Kick in your resilient response with intention and an unbeatable desire to overcome your current situation. Ask yourself, why might this negative situation be the best thing that ever happened to me? How might this moment prepare me to do better for the rest of my life?

7. LEARN HOW TO BE PATIENT WITH JUSTIN

" You have to get that edge of always wanting something more. My work ethic came from a need within me to exceed expectations."

— JUSTIN

P-utting
A-ppropriate
T-imelines
I-nto
E-nthusiastic,
N-on-stop
T-raining

———

Mindset conversations tend to be action-based. Setting goals, being motivated, and acting on those motivations are certainly a huge part of a positive, forward-moving mindset. Patience, however, tends to get left out of those conversations. It may be the most important factor in a person's mindset and their ability to achieve the results they hope for. Sometimes, goals will not come to fruition for years. Patience is the bridge that connects a strong mindset to a large, long-term goal. Without it, many have quit too early or sought out easier successes instead of waiting for their true desires. Justin did not fall victim to impatience. With time and consistency, he positioned himself to reach his biggest goals.

Meet Justin

A man with a plan, Justin entered his freshman year of high school with a vision of what his life would be like after high school. He committed to a life, a career, and most importantly, to the small steps he could take at that time to help him reach those goals. A desire burned in him to become a firefighter and a leader in every aspect of his life. He knew that it would be a long journey with a variety of challenges. Embracing those obstacles, he began the process early of becoming the man he wanted to be.

Justin was one of the most surprising student-athletes I have ever worked with. He entered school as a small, scrawny, goofy young man. He had a joke for every situation and seemed to take nothing seriously. I was prepared to pour extra effort into him because I thought he would need to do a lot of growing up. Little did I know, behind the laughter and silliness, Justin had a very serious mission and a quiet but clear determination to accomplish it.

Adversities in Stride

While Justin had a solid idea in his mind of where his life would head, he knew that he would face adversity throughout the process. He embraced those opportunities and knew how to compartmentalize them in his head. Each moment of difficulty would be a step that brought him closer to his goal. That concept lodged firmly in mind as he entered high school with a long journey to go.

Justin's journey started with difficulty in the classroom. While his grades were excellent, he had to overcome the challenge of reading out loud in class. He explained, "when I would read out loud, I would get so nervous. It would cause me to stutter. Kids would make fun of me for it, and it would shake my confidence and make me stutter even more." Confidence was going to be a key to his success, so he knew it was a must to overcome his issues with stuttering. He continued challenging himself to read out loud and face those fears, knowing that the laughter of his classmates would only add fuel to him overcoming this obstacle.

As Justin took the task of reading out loud head-on, he was faced with a second challenge in the form of a difficult new sport. He had joined the wrestling team. From the beginning, it felt like he had hit a wall quickly. His workout partners were more experienced and much stronger. His matches would be dictated by his nerves. Being overexcited, he would accidentally work himself out of position and give his calmer opponents easy advantages. He began to compile disappointing losses on the mat to add to the confidence-crushing moments in the classroom.

A new approach was needed. Justin told me, "I learned not to worry about the outcome now. Work towards that mess-up I had and do what I have to do to buckle down to strive to get into what I want to do. Use my mistakes to get better." He spent the majority of his Freshman year trying to understand how those early mistakes and let-downs could lead him to be better. He knew that the fire academy would require a much tougher, more confident young man. With this knowledge, he began to express gratitude for every obstacle in his path.

When Justin began his sophomore year, I could already see a new and improved version of him. He walked in brimming with confidence and talking like a champion. He was ready to crush it in school and sports. A renewed effort was marked by extra practices, more workouts, and increased participation in classes. He didn't want to be a great athlete or a great student. He wanted to be a great person of character. The extra steps he took were meant to build his character in the way he saw fit. This effort worked well to his advantage until the next adversity struck.

Putting Plan to Action

Justin had an advantage that many do not, in the form of a large and powerful support system. He was surrounded by encouraging family and friends who were able to lift him up whenever he felt like he had crashed. Leading this charge was his father, a successful and generous man of character. Justin's father modeled the attitude that he wanted to incorporate, and led him on that path. Just when the mentorship and wisdom were beginning to kick into overdrive, Justin's dad fell ill.

It was like a slow-motion button had been pressed on Justin's life. Where he was once making strides, his progress became stagnant. Hospital trips and long nights at home marked his school year. He said, "My dad pushed me a lot to succeed. He made me want to be a better person in every aspect of life. I wanted to get noticed as a high school student." The sudden onset of his father's illness shifted Justin's priorities away from those goals and towards caring for his family.

It was an unremarkable year by Justin's standards as his academic and athletic endeavors took a backseat. However, one thing became clear. Justin could not rely on his family to turn him into the man he wanted to be. He had to be willing to take that journey on his own and succeed through his patience and determination. One day at a time, he became more invested in his own success. He applied a consistent effort in striving toward his goals, becoming even more involved in school clubs and adding swimming to the sports he would compete in. It was time for Justin to see what would happen if he applied every lesson his dad taught him with full intensity and effort.

Thankfully, Justin's father had a successful recovery. The mental block that had once held Justin back was lifted. His final years of high school were not met with championships and earth-shattering victories. They were met with what he really needed, continuous upward trajectory. Each semester led to a slight raising in his GPA. Every swimming tournament portrayed a faster individual time for him. His wrestling success was drastically improved, leading to his best two seasons and a deep run into the postseason.

All of the success Justin received was right on track for what he needed. He knew that he would have to come out of high school prepared for a demanding, life-on-the-line job. He was now that man. He stood as a physically fit, mentally tough, character-driven man who was used to a consistent effort and an ability to grow through any challenge. Along with the impressive resume of involvement and activities that he had gathered, his persistence and patience allowed him to be an early entrant to EMT school and the fire academy.

Testing Patience

A great deal of care was taken by Justin in developing the traits he would need beyond his schooling. However, those qualities would still be tested. He entered the EMT program and began working through it shortly after his high school graduation. Diving right in, he would find a whole new level of challenge in succeeding at this level. He failed his first attempt at his big exam. A second attempt met the same result. The question began to pop up in his head: was he ready for this?

"I really had to check my motivation," he explained. After high school, he felt like he had put in the work and prepared enough that things would be a walk in the park. Failing showed Justin how important it would be for him to continue to produce the effort that had led to his success in the past. He doubled down on his efforts and studied harder than he had in high school. He took extra tutoring and looked for help from previous students who had been successful. This effort led him to his third attempt, which was his last opportunity to pass before requiring remedial classes. Not only did he pass it, but he also raised his score by a significant amount.

The experience helped Justin to develop even more patience and consistency. These were not traits he could take for granted. Rather, discipline was a gift that, when utilized, allowed him to accomplish anything he dreamed of. As he continued through EMT and fire academy, he brought those foundational principles to the front of his mind. The discipline and patience that he had developed would become the currency that could buy his success at any level.

Entering Justin Into the Perfect Ten

I did not realize how driven Justin was from the start of his high school career. I misjudged his relaxed nature for a lack of seriousness. At first, I thought his goals were to just survive a season of wrestling. I did not see the foresight he had of reaching his real dream of becoming a successful firefighter. He was ten steps ahead of his peers and even ahead of his teachers and coaches in terms of maturity. Masked behind a silly smile, young Justin was on a path that only he knew.

Slowly, it dawned on me that Justin was building to something bigger. The defining moment where it sank in for me was in his senior year. I had watched him patiently await his opportunities and work quietly to be in a position to succeed. He managed several upset victories in wrestling to make it to "the bloodround," which is the nickname for the match to either make it to the state championship or be eliminated from the tournament. Seizing every opportunity, he fought his hardest and came up short to a very skilled opponent. When he returned to the bleachers, we spoke about the end of his wrestling career. He simply shrugged his shoulders and said, "I am proud of the effort I put in and the results I got out. I got what I needed out of this sport."

Perfection to him did not mean a certain level of achievement. It was about growing the foundation to be able to meet his bigger life goals. He knew that he didn't have to win as much as he had to improve. He forced himself into a cycle of punishing, challenging conditions for him to overcome and surpass. This cycle gave him the perfect opportunity to take control of his life and future.

My New Definition of the Perfect Student

The perfect student:

- Hustles harder than their peers because of an unyielding passion that they possess.
- Embraces their identity, honoring and valuing the unique qualities and passions that they possess.
- Has an unyielding mental toughness that pushes them past any barrier or limitation that stands in their way.
- Knows how to remain optimistic and apply it to their everyday lives.
- Is committed to bouncing back and remaining resilient, no matter what happens to them.
- **Remains patient and works steadily and consistently towards their goals.**

Your New Definition of the Perfect Student

Did this chapter impact your definition of a perfect student? How important does patience rank when considering the strengths of a student? Flip back to the introduction and look over your first definition. Reflect on what you said and what you read. Is your definition firm, or is it shifting? Write down your reflections in this space, or continue revising your definition:

Mindset Lesson

Patience cannot be developed in a day. This is a skill that will require constant practice and work. By nature, patience is built from putting off the short term "feel-goods" for long-term improvement. The more patient you become, the more effort you will be able to apply to your daily efforts of improvement.

Justin believed that patience was easier to develop when breaking big tasks up into smaller segments. He described, "I would take each day in three categories. Go all out in school. During practice, I would go all out. Then, I would go all out on work. If I didn't have work that day, I knew I could rest and give an even stronger effort the next day." He never worried about the entirety of his schedule or the many things he had to accomplish each day. He simply focused on one thing at a time and separated that task out from the rest. This narrow focus allowed him to be patient without feeling overwhelmed by the many activities he participated in.

Here are five ways to improve your patience:

1. Have a long-term goal that is driven by the character and attitude you will need
2. Break your long-term goals into short, daily tasks to accomplish
3. Write out your schedule and stay in the moment for whatever your current task is
4. Measure your results by growth, not by numbers or grades or trophies
5. Tell your support system about your long-term goals and utilize their help in moving toward those goals

Overlooking Patience

How often do we see people who seem to be casual, relaxed, and unbothered? It can be frustrating to see patient people because they do not appear to be in a hurry often. In Justin's case, he became one of the most accomplished student-athletes I have ever worked with. I would not have guessed that early on in his career, because I underestimated how patient he could remain in keeping his sights locked onto his goals.

Do not make the mistake that I almost made. Ask people about their vision. Work to understand what drives them. Many of us get caught up in the moment, focusing only on what is right in front of us. Learn to create conversations around long-term thoughts and bigger ideas. You will incorporate patient people into your life and understand them more by standing by their side, looking towards the vision they are building toward each day.

Make it Yours

It is difficult to be patient, but even more so if there is nothing that seems worth it for you to be patient for. As you wrap up this chapter, begin to reflect on your long-term vision. It doesn't matter what your age is. Based on where you are right now in life, where do you want to be? How long might it take you to get there? What kind of person do you want to develop into? What is your mission?

As you come up with answers for that, you will be able to think of smaller steps that will lead you to the person you will need to be for future success. Make the small steps the big deal. Continue to make progress and put your whole heart into your daily work. The more you forge ahead, the easier patience will become as you progress towards your big achievement.

8. LEARN HOW TO BE KIND WITH EMILY

" When you give to others you get more. That's how I've always been.

I'm always smiling at people because I don't know if they are having a bad day."

— EMILY

K-eeping an
I-ntent to
N-urture
D-elightfulness

———

It is often said that success is selfish. There may be some truth to that statement, insofar as a person needs to care about their own journey and fight for their best opportunities to achieve. However, another perspective exists on this matter. A person can elevate their own success by elevating others. Achievement does not need to come in isolation or in competition with others. Some people find greatness in their own lives by helping and serving others. Kindness can be a recipe for success, as this next student learned very early on.

Meet Emily

Emily was raised by a large, loving family in the Dominican Republic. Her childhood saw a model of hard work and gratitude. Her parents both worked extremely hard to provide a positive life for her, and showed gratitude for all of the opportunities they received to succeed in that mission. Her father was a restaurant owner in the D.R., and her mother ran a salon out of their house. Emily was tasked with helping around the house to sustain her parents' busy schedules. She quickly adopted the attitude of hustle, needing to help around the house to ensure a strong, functioning family unit.

Her family moved to the United States and applied the same practice of hard work and gratitude that made them successful in the D.R. They sought out every opportunity to provide for their family while remaining thankful for the new life they were building in a new place. Emily brought with her the foundation of faith and family, two guiding principles that led her every step. She believed that she could create a positive future and follow the example that her family had set. With a variety of challenges looming, her ability to think positively and embody that strong work ethic would be put to the test.

Prioritizing, but not Passing

A clear set of priorities emerged as Emily began her high school career. Her main focus was to be kind, become a positive force for the people around her, and live out the faith she had in God. She would often be seen in the hallways with an ear to ear smile, greeting friends and strangers with the same level of enthusiasm. A patient listener, she would give time to anyone and display a genuine curiosity in wanting to know more about them. She quickly became known as a helper, a friend, and a kind face for anyone who needed encouragement. While this kindness opened her up to many circles and surrounded her with positive thinkers, an issue emerged at school. Her grades did not reflect the warm, caring persona that she brought to the classroom.

Emily's family was strongly character-driven. However, their challenging work schedules left little time for them to keep track of her performance. She explained, "My brother didn't graduate. My parents didn't monitor grades much in high school or help with homework. They only checked the report cards." Emily's school performance was not hopeless, but she had placed herself early on as a risk to not graduate. Several failed classes began to pile up and burden her daily schedule.

The struggles Emily faced in school were not from a lack of trying or from low attendance. She would work extremely hard, yet it would seemingly get her nowhere. She said, "I've never been the school person. I always wanted to learn things by seeing and doing but struggled with interest and didn't want to read or do science. I could never focus, and I could see other kids and go, how did they focus and I couldn't?" Her frustration became clear as year after year, her friends advanced and seemed to have very little difficulty with content that felt both uninter-esting and complex to her. It happened quietly and slowly, but her chances of graduating became slimmer with each quarter that passed.

Reaping the Rewards of Kindness

A mountain of work stood in between Emily and the success she had hoped for. Teetering around the minimum GPA for graduation and short several credits, she knew that change was needed. What she did not realize immediately was the support system that she had created for herself. On top of the encouragement of her family, she had teachers, counselors, and a gathering of friends who all wanted to see her succeed. She had spent the first few years in high school serving, leading, and loving others. Now, it was time for that kindness to come back to her when she needed it most.

School subjects did not become any less difficult for her, but the motivation and belief in her ability to graduate were restored. She said,

Counselors scared the crap out of me. Seeing my brother not graduate, I didn't want to do the same thing and disappoint my parents. They expected to see us walk the stage and you know what, he didn't do it, so I'll get it. Don't worry guys I'll walk the stage and you'll see me. That drove me to step up.

Her motivation went through the roof as she stared at the extra classes, make-up work, and difficult lectures that stood in her way of graduating.

As her motivation raised, she began to receive extra help and informal tutoring from me. While she graciously gave me much of the credit for her success, what stood out most was why I was helping her. Like most teachers, I was always strapped for time, wishing I could help my students more but being unable to accomplish it. However, I always found time for Emily, because she had found time for me first.

Beginning in her freshman year, Emily would take time out of her day to clean my classroom, organize my desk, and file my paperwork. I never asked her to; she would just do it. When I asked her why, she would explain that I was a teacher and I deserved respect and a clean work-space. Throughout the years and as my family grew, Emily would check in on me to make sure my family had everything we needed and that my classroom was in order. She even refused to take service hours from me for all of the help she gave me.

Helping me had become one of many examples in her life where Emily's kindness reaped a future benefit. I was an all-in supporter of her success. I would not rest until she graduated. Often, she would sit in my class to get an extra English lesson or a science refresher. It was common for me to check her homework, hold her accountable to her schedule, and monitor her grades. Along with the help she received from her friends and counselors, this would be the push she needed. Her dedicated cast of supporters would get to join her family in watching her walk down the stage for graduation.

Entering Emily Into the Perfect Ten

It would be difficult for a traditional-minded person to place Emily as a "perfect student." Her grades were constantly in tension with her boredom. She was unfocused and inconsistent throughout her classroom years. Many of the typical traits of perfection were out the window with her.

I had always believed in Emily as a wonderful student, but it became incredibly clear as I watched her transition to working life. Each job that she held would constantly promote her, giving her opportunities beyond her peers and employees who held age and experience over her. I asked her how she opened up those opportunities, and she explained,

Being the person that I am gets eyes on me. I stand out from everyone else which is what businesses want. I say hi to everyone and all managers know me by my name in every department and I'm the only one they say hi to. I go out of my way to do that because they matter too even if they are in a different department. That helps with opportunity.

The skills that Emily learned in high school were not entirely academic in nature, but they have served her well. She learned to show consistent kindness and really listen to people. She can make anybody feel like the most important person in the world as they talk to her. Utilizing that skill made the difference for her graduation, the friendships she gained, the network she established, and the life opportunities she continues to receive. She applied what she learned from her family and what she believed in God to become a well-rounded young woman capable of accomplishing anything!

My New Definition of the Perfect Student

The perfect student:

- Hustles harder than their peers because of an unyielding passion that they possess.
- Embraces their identity, honoring and valuing the unique qualities and passions that they possess.
- Has an unyielding mental toughness that pushes them past any barrier or limitation that stands in their way.
- Knows how to remain optimistic and apply it to their everyday lives.
- Is committed to bouncing back and remaining resilient, no matter what happens to them.
- Remains patient and works steadily and consistently towards their goals.
- **Shows genuine kindness and seeks to serve others freely.**

Your New Definition of the Perfect Student

Did this chapter impact your definition of a perfect student? How important does kindness rank when considering the strengths of a student? Flip back to the introduction and look over your first definition. Reflect on what you said and what you read. Is your definition firm, or is it shifting? Write down your reflections in this space, or continue revising your definition:

Mindset Lesson

Kindness is a creator of opportunities. It is a piece of your mindset that can always be grown and developed, but it cannot be faked. Real kindness has the ability to lift others up and encourage them to rise beyond their current self-perceptions. A commitment to serving, understanding, and leading others is a necessary beginning to true kindness.

Emily believed that leadership and self-love were crucial aspects of kindness. She gave the following advice:

Try to be a leader and not a follower. People want to follow everyone else but you need to learn to be you. Be your own person. Learn to accept yourself and accept others. Love yourself because if you can't you won't love anyone else. Don't judge. None of us have any right to judge anyone. Don't try to impress someone else. If they aren't impressed then they aren't meant for you.

Becoming a leader starts with leading your own life. As you allow yourself to stand out, you will be in a better position to serve and love others. Like Emily, this will spread kindness that is much more likely to return to you tenfold.

Here are five steps you can take to improve your kindness:

1. Learn people's names and how to say them properly
2. Go out of your way to greet people, especially strangers or people who are not in your immediate circle
3. Ask specific questions beyond the typical "how's it going?" Give people your time and full attention when they answer you
4. Look for opportunities to serve in your family, friend group, and community to make someone else's life easier
5. Write down positive notes to yourself and be your own number one encourager

Overlooking the Kind

Students like Emily often get overlooked due to their demeanor. Kind, compassionate people are likely to become stuck in the role of having to help others., Many people will dump their problems and concerns on kind people because of their good-hearted nature. Likewise, many do not worry about offending or irritating kind people, knowing that they will forgive and forget.

Do not fall into the trap of underestimating the power of a kind person. Kindness spreads kindness, so they will want to surround themselves with other compassionate people. Instead of laying your problems into your kind friends, repay their kindness with yours. Act in service and allow yourself to be a positive influence to those who are being a positive influence to you.

Make it Yours

It is easy to allow other people's successes to feel like failures to you. Comparing yourself to others may become a dangerous roadblock to kindness. Accepting a more kind demeanor means dropping judgments and jealousy for a much more preferable outcome. Be a strong advocate for yourself and a prepared supporter for others.

The goal of kindness is to be consistent, not purposeful. Purposeful kindness is the type that seeks gain out of acting kind. If you are only nice to those who can benefit you immediately, you miss out on many long-term opportunities or relationships that could have made a positive impact on your life. Ask yourself if your kindness comes with a price, or if you give willingly. Does a kind demeanor exemplify the character you want to have? What value can you add to the life of your family, friends, or strangers? What are you willing to give and how are you willing to serve simply to be a positive influence on the world?

9. LEARN HOW TO BE CONFIDENT WITH BRADEN

> The day you learn to ignore what people say and love yourself is the day where you can truly be your best. You no longer worry about people's opinions, the voices of judgment fade away. The ones that unconditionally support you become easier to hear."

— BRADEN

C-reating
O-pportunities
N-uanced
F-rom
I-ndividual,
D-istinctive
E-lements with a
N-onchalant
T-emperment

———

A confident disposition can change the way that people perceive you. More importantly, it can change the way you view yourself. Confidence is the ability to believe the best in yourself. People who are confident know that they can learn, grow, and rise above any challenge. They do not necessarily believe that they are the best, but they do believe that they have the potential for greatness. Confidence was the difference-maker that changed the course of Braden's life.

Meet Braden

Braden is the son of two outstanding educators. He described himself as half White and half Colombian. He was tall and skinny, but athletic in his own right. As his teacher in both middle school and high school, I had the unique opportunity to remember a small period of time when he was around my height, before he sprouted above six feet tall and towered over me. His personality was that of a young stand-up comic. He was always smiling, laughing, joking, and coming up with unique observations.

Braden's personality would get him in minor trouble at times. His jokes often gave him the reputation of being class clown, and his observations would lead to many small classroom interruptions. However, laughing and joking served an important purpose to him. He explained,

Humor was my escape through the hardest times in school but not because it made me laugh but because it made others laugh. There were days where it felt like I was at a new rock bottom and those days I would watch stand up, hearing the jokes and stories that the comics would tell always helped me feel better and forget about my troubles.

Braden's motivation to joke around was purposeful in that he was using it to cope. He told silly stories and made people laugh to help them avoid feeling the way that he felt. The positive impact he brought to others was the same positive force he needed in his own life.

Hiding Confidence

Behind his warm and welcoming smile, Braden was downplaying his potential in a great way. He seemed confident because of how outgoing he was, but he wasn't exactly himself. There was a piece of him that seemed off. It would come out with the occasional deprecating humor where he would put himself down. It could be heard in the way he would hype up his friends by saying that he could never do the things they did. Little by little, his seemingly confident nature diminished.

With his personality slowly fading, Braden began reflecting on his level of confidence. He wondered why he couldn't live up to the potential that his parents, teachers, and friends saw in him. As he faced many small challenges in school, he began to realize that his relationships were impacting the perception he had of himself. He said,

It took my first heartbreak to develop my confidence. I would routinely think to myself that I wasn't good enough and that's why everything happened, but over time I started to see that I went above and beyond on my side of the relationship and that I am worth a lot more than this person made me feel.

It took time for Braden to break free of the thinking that somebody else could determine his own level of confidence. He continued his schooling, going through the motions but not seeming to find his bearings. As he dealt with heartbreak, he began to get involved in more sports. Friends had prompted him to become more involved on campus.

Braden's hilarious sense of humor made him a great addition to every-thing he joined, but he still hadn't put the pieces of his confidence together yet.

Laughing through Pain

Braden's path through high school had become smoother. He was doing well enough in school to move forward with little trouble. His athletic performances were finding a groove, especially in volleyball. Socially, he had made his way around many circles, casting a wide web of friendship with his dynamic personality. His confidence was slowly building him into a person who believed in himself. That was when tragedy struck.

Like many of his classmates, Braden would have his dreams and goals shaken up by devastating events that happened among his circle. Within a fairly short period of time, he would go through the passing of some of his close friends. Not long after, the shooting at a neighboring school, Marjory Stoneman Douglas, would shock him even further. He described,

I learned that life doesn't care where you're at, it will test you more than any other teacher will. Life will beat you to the ground and keep you there if you let it. With the loss of multiple close friends and my first experience with really feeling at my lowest point, I had to learn that life is about fighting through adversity and working hard to be your best even through hard times."

It was difficult for Braden to carry on with confidence as he faced the very real trauma of loss. School returned to normal, but he had a tremendous weight on his shoulders due to the losses he had experienced. There was little time left in high school for Braden to make his mark and become the man that many believed he could be. He would have to keep striving for that goal through heartbreak and loss.

Going for the Block

In volleyball, a team will try to spike the ball at the other team. Tall, athletic players will jump up and attempt to block the quickly moving ball as it crosses over the net. As Braden got deeper into volleyball, he began to make big blocks on the court and in his life. The tragedies, the breakups, and the challenges of life were on the attack, but he was ready to jump up, block them, and score some points of his own.

The last stretch of Braden's high school career showed a reinvigorated, confident, relentless warrior. He was no longer a young boy who put himself down to build up others. He was a man of responsibility and action, ready to conquer every challenge in front of him. With added confidence, he positioned himself to become a leader.

The interesting thing about his confidence was that he didn't have to change his personality. He still cracked jokes throughout the day and brought smiles to many of his classmates' (and teachers') faces. He kept finding ways to enjoy life and challenge himself. He was not a new person. What changed was his approach as he engaged in each task. He was incredibly focused in class, only making jokes after he had learned, practiced, and absorbed each piece of material. He put his entire heart into volleyball, pushing himself to a level beyond what he expected. The value he placed on friendships led him to be even more caring and empathetic.

Braden explained that the love he developed for volleyball led him to success in other areas of his life.

The drive I had for volleyball was a huge part of it. Volleyball is my passion and I knew that it didn't matter how good I was at volleyball. Without good grades, I wasn't going to find a college that wanted me. I wouldn't have been happy if I couldn't have taken volleyball to the next level so I did everything I could to make sure I had the best chance to continue doing what I love.

With support from his family and encouragement from his friends, he pushed towards his goal with every last ounce of effort he had. By the end of his senior year, he held in his hand a world of opportunity and the prize he had worked for tirelessly: a college scholarship.

Entering Braden Into the Perfect Ten

Braden was the student who I could not discipline in class. It was a regular occasion for him to test my "I can't punish you if I laugh" rule. His puns would make every vocabulary lesson interesting and unexpected. He stood out in many positive ways, yet I also saw a young man who wasn't living up to the person he could be. I also saw the dedication he put into making sure his friends were excelling and creating amazing opportunities for themselves. I had wished for many years that he could believe in himself in the way that he did everyone else.

I knew that he had found himself from both his performance on the volleyball court and in his school performance. A switch had flipped in his mind. He was ready to accept the difficulties of life and overcome them wholeheartedly. Earning a scholarship with only three years of experience in the sport, he proved that his confidence could carry him to any level.

Entering Braden into the "Perfect Ten" can be summed up by this thought from him: "I have a desire for progression. I'm not the kind of person who enjoys being in the same situation for a long time. I want things to move forward and get bigger and better." He had made a transformation from hoping things would get better, to believing they could, to acting on the belief that they would. As he pushed for progress, his confidence led him well outside of his comfort zone and into a constant flow of growth.

My New Definition of the Perfect Student

The perfect student:

- Hustles harder than their peers because of an unyielding passion that they possess.
- Embraces their identity, honoring and valuing the unique qualities and passions that they possess.
- Has an unyielding mental toughness that pushes them past any barrier or limitation that stands in their way.

- Knows how to remain optimistic and apply it to their everyday lives.
- Is committed to bouncing back and remaining resilient, no matter what happens to them.
- Remains patient and works steadily and consistently towards their goals.
- Shows genuine kindness and seeks to serve others freely.
- **Is confident in their ability to learn, progress, and reach new levels.**

Your New Definition of the Perfect Student

Did this chapter impact your definition of a perfect student? How important does confidence rank when considering the strengths of a student? Flip back to the introduction and look over your first definition. Reflect on what you said and what you read. Is your definition firm, or is it shifting? Write down your reflections in this space, or continue revising your definition:

Mindset Lesson

A popular perception exists that confidence is an inherent trait that you either have or do not have. This perception provides an easy way out. For many, it is easier to shrug their shoulders and believe they do not have the skill, rather than practicing and working towards that skill. Confidence can be practiced, attained, and grown from any level.

Braden offered this advice to anyone looking to build their confidence as he did:

Do what you love. Find the passion that really drives you to be your best, something that tests you physically, mentally, and spiritually. A true passion will push you past what you thought you were even capable of. Be your most true self, regardless of what anybody else thinks.

As other students have offered throughout this book, he credited passion as a way to leverage and build confidence.

Following Braden's advice, here are five ways to build your confidence:

1. Write down a list of your passions, hobbies, and interests
2. Write down (and follow through on) steps that you can take to bring those interests to a higher level, or further outside of your comfort zone
3. When family and friends support, encourage, and compliment you, begin asking yourself, "what if they are right about me?"
4. Know your personality strengths and rely on them when you feel doubt
5. Do not give permission to anybody except yourself in defining your worth and ability

Overlooking Confidence

Face-to-face with a student like Braden, it is easy to assume that they will win at everything. Whenever I heard the rare moment where Braden would lose a volleyball game, I would have a hard time believing it. How could someone brimming with confidence ever face defeat? This ideology is where many confident people become overlooked.

A strong sense of confidence allows students to overcome failures and use them as experience. Honing in on failures and making a big deal out of them can sap the confidence out of anyone. Remember that confident people are not worried about results as much as they are focused on performing to their best ability. If you believe a student's confidence to automatically equal their success at everything, you run the risk of devaluing the experience they need in favor of the results that should not matter to them.

Make it Yours

How hard are you willing to work to become more confident? It typically requires a heavy dose of discomfort. Confidence is rarely built in solitude and within the things that make you comfortable. Utilize your passions to build confidence in moments of discomfort and pressure.

While you seek to build confidence, be sure to find role models, mentors, and even peers who model a strong level of confidence. Spot people who constantly believe in themselves and never count themselves out. Take note of their characteristics. How do they hold their posture when standing and sitting? What types of words and phrases do they use to describe themselves? How do they react when something gives them difficulty? Watch for those cues and apply them to your life. Confidence is key to unlocking the person you can become.

10. LEARN HOW TO BE RESPONSIBLE WITH VIC

" Use whatever people say bad about you to your positive benefit. If you grab onto everything negative and hang on to it, you will be stuck in your bubble of sadness."

— Vic

R-esponding to
E-very
S-ituation
P-oised,
O-ffering
N-oticeable
S-olutions
I-nstantly
B-y
L-imiting
E-xcuses

———

R esponsibility is a rarely discussed yet powerful aspect of a person's mindset. Having a sense of responsibility can fend off procrastination and create forward momentum towards any task. Responsible people keep track of what they need to do, and they do not accept any excuse that prevents them from completing those tasks. It is a skill that can elevate the performance of any student. Even more so, having a strong sense of responsibility can create opportunities in work and life while creating a trustworthy and dependable image of oneself. For Vic, responsibility became the glue that held her life, her studies, and her dreams together.

Meet Vic

Vic was born and raised in New Jersey by her Latin family. Fluent in English and Portuguese, she grew up as a high achieving student. Her potential was through the roof in many aspects, and her ability to learn was incredible. Her studiousness was supplemented by her kind and understanding demeanor. She was full of curiosity and always willing to listen and learn from the stories and experiences of others.

While she developed a variety of strong academic skills, much of that was done through hardships and challenges at home. The trials her family went through would overshadow her progress in school. A positive-minded girl, Vic focused on her growth and fought to stay on track. Struggling to keep up in school, she would find the responsibility of graduating as a nearly impossible mountain to climb.

Battling through the Barriers

While Vic was born in New Jersey, her parents had recently immigrated to the country. Immigration came with sacrifice and challenge as they looked for work, housing, and consistency. This led to many long nights and late hours of work, leaving Vic to manage herself and complete her studies. The pressure of an unstable financial situation led her father down a path of drinking for relief.

As their situation worsened, her family made the decision to move and gain a fresh start. In Florida, they began to find their rhythm as a family. Vic's dad was able to recover and begin to restore the relationships that had been damaged. Vic had endured days of hunger and uncertainty about the safety of her family, but things had seemed to settle. The move brought a sense of peace and prosperity over her that carried into her excellent school work. She explained, "All that negativity, I would put into a positive form. Positivity is the only thing that will get you through life."

Knocked Off the Tracks

Entering high school, it would have been difficult to guess that Vic had been through so many tough experiences. She was well put together, constantly smiling, and exuberant in class. Her schedule filled quickly with honors and advanced placement courses. She thrived in her friend group, contributing and encouraging others to succeed. As a freshman, she was poised to receive a great number of accolades in the school. Report cards came and went, displaying good news for her family to see. That is until the whirlwind hit.

It happened all so suddenly. Vic's life became entangled in a variety of setbacks in the blink of an eye. Continuing her high school career, she faced her most difficult schedule. Her decision to challenge herself with advanced classes had shaken her confidence. That confidence was further derailed by a passing moment that she described, "a teacher said that because I'm Hispanic, I won't be anything. It dropped my self-esteem a lot. Teachers are supposed to bring you up, not down, and I just couldn't live up to what the teacher wanted." The bright-eyed, always cheerful Vic had gone quiet and reserved.

While classes presented challenges of their own, her social life had taken a major hit as well. The friends she had started off high school with had disappeared. The strong social bonds she had created were broken off quickly. Gossip, rumors, and cliques had left her in the dust. She found solace in her dating life, meeting a boy who was loyal and understanding to her. However, even that became a challenge as her time and priorities began to shift towards him and away from studying for the classes that had become intensely difficult for her.

Between classes and a boyfriend, a new responsibility was added in the form of work. Needing to contribute financially to her family, Vic began to apply for jobs around the community. Her work schedule began to interfere with her studying time and, more importantly, her sleep. The demands of earning a paycheck had become overwhelming and left very little energy for her to succeed during the day.

Noticing the change, Vic's mom had many conversations with her about the importance of school and grades. Conversations became small quarrels, which became big arguments. Her home life had once again become a difficult place for her to gather her thoughts and move forward. The pressure of school and work had left her very little time to even be at home, let alone to unwind, rest, and recover.

With the whirlwind of a difficult schedule with teachers who did not understand her, a social life in disarray, work hours that were nearly impossible to keep, and a home life marked with conflict, Vic's grades took a toll. She was sinking. The change between years was drastic. It was clear that she had crashed under the weight of teenage life and school pressure. Along with her grades, her personality became more withdrawn and isolated. It seemed like she had fallen completely off her original path. From honors classes a year ago, she was now on track to drop out.

Rebuilding with Responsibility

Entering her senior year, Vic almost seemed like a lost cause. Her credits had fallen behind, her work schedule had only gotten more demanding, and her life was as hectic as always. A debate raged in her head about her goals. She wrestled with the idea of dropping out. She said, "I didn't think I was going to graduate. Around December, I was ready to call it; there's no way I can make this happen. My school counselor said I would not make it to graduation day." With a plethora of credits to obtain and a busy life, graduation seemed like an impossible goal.

Facing the end of her student life, Vic made a choice. It was time to embrace the responsibilities she had. One responsibility was to graduate and she was going to make it happen. She pulled all of her resources and energy, pouring every ounce of it into her schoolwork to begin the recovery process. She explained, "I did homework at work. I took lots of Starbucks double shots. I started Multitasking, always staying productive at school." She understood the value of time as graduation loomed closer, so she vowed to not waste a minute of it.

Slowly, the Vic I had met as a freshman reemerged. She was clearly tired, but she began to look more like herself. She was talking positively, believing in herself, finding a way back on top of her work, and acting like the student she had always been capable of being. Courses were recovered one by one. Eventually, she had found herself on the list of students expected to graduate. The grind of catching up and the multitasking at her jobs had finally paid dividends. She was able to walk with her peers and receive her diploma with pride, having overcome the trials of school and life while living out the responsibilities she had set.

Entering Vic Into the Perfect Ten

Vic's high school career could have been defined as a total breakdown of her potential. Her smarts were quickly overshadowed by the variety of obstacles that crushed her. Her story was marred by setbacks and challenges that got the best of her in many ways. That is why she is a part of my "Perfect Ten."

For many students, the pressure is to stay on a perfect path and act like nothing can bother them. Well, many things bothered Vic. They pushed her to the very end of her high school career. She was able to use all of those moments to develop a stronger sense of responsibility and a heightened motivation to overcome these barriers to her success. Every failure became another reason why she would succeed and come out better. Her path became perfect for creating the woman she is now, prepared to take on any of life's difficulties while brushing off the doubts and criticisms of others. She explained it best when she said, "It felt good to shake the hand of the school counselor who told me I would not graduate, on the stage at graduation day."

Vic may have lost sight of her goals momentarily, but she never lost sight of the responsibility she had to herself. She knew that she wanted to be a college-educated, professional woman. The way she achieved it was unexpected, but her journey has continued successfully in college as she continues to live out her life, responsible to the person she wants to become.

My New Definition of the Perfect Student

The perfect student:

- Hustles harder than their peers because of an unyielding passion that they possess.
- Embraces their identity, honoring and valuing the unique qualities and passions that they possess.
- Has an unyielding mental toughness that pushes them past any barrier or limitation that stands in their way.
- Knows how to remain optimistic and apply it to their everyday lives.
- Is committed to bouncing back and remaining resilient, no matter what happens to them.
- Remains patient and works steadily and consistently towards

their goals.
- Shows genuine kindness and seeks to serve others freely.
- Is confident in their ability to learn, progress, and reach new levels.
- **Holds themselves responsible and finds a way to complete the tasks they have set out to do.**

Your New Definition of the Perfect Student

Did this chapter impact your definition of a perfect student? How important does responsibility rank when considering the strengths of a student? Flip back to the introduction and look over your first definition. Reflect on what you said and what you read. Is your definition firm, or is it shifting? Write down your reflections in this space, or continue revising your definition:

Mindset Lesson

Responsibility comes with a set of standards. To be responsible, it is first important to understand what your standards of success are. When you know the person you are working towards becoming, it will not matter what obstacles present themselves that might throw your life off track. You will be able to come back to the person you are growing to be. Responsibility is a serious trait that carries weight and importance with it. When you accept responsibility, no excuse can be given to shirk it.

Vic gave advice regarding responsibility. Her tip was,

Set your goals straight. I started mapping out what my future looked like, not a week from now or at the end of the school year. I Thought 10 years forward and used that to motivate myself.

It was important for her to have a guiding vision that she could rely on in times of trouble. That way, she knew exactly what needed to be done to recover and maintain her responsibilities.

Here are five ways you can add to your sense of responsibility:

1. Have a clear vision of who you want to be in the future
2. Identify the positive supports you have in life and go to them early and often
3. Change negative comments that people make about you into positive statements of power
4. Write down your common excuses and be aware of what you tend to say to avoid responsibilities
5. Refuse to feel sorry for yourself and embrace every obstacle that you face with the knowledge that it will help you grow

Overlooking the Responsible

Responsibility can be difficult. It can equate to late nights, long stretches of hard work, and simply not enough naps. For Vic, it did not always appear that she had it together. However, her trait of responsibility always ensured that she would find a way to come out on top. Behind the girl who was racing from school to job, clearly lacking sleep, there stood a driven girl with a plan and a method to succeed with no excuses.

Do not assume that a student who is in a bind is irresponsible or lacking a desire to succeed. Many responsible students take on more than they can handle by the nature of relying on their responsibility. It may appear that they are drowning in their work. Ask them about their plans. Help them with their efficiency. Provide them strategies, or at least be a sounding board for them, as they determine the best possible way to meet the many responsibilities they have been tasked with.

Make it Yours

Have you built a strong sense of responsibility in your life? Do you hold yourself accountable to the person you want to become? No matter what your circumstances are, it is important to set boundaries to protect the person you are building towards. Having a clear vision and a lack of excuses will give you the power needed to remain responsible to yourself.

As you consider responsibility, learn to forgive your mistakes and forgo dwelling too long on the negative situations that have happened in your life. If you find yourself thinking about the things that hold you back, use it to reinforce how cool it will be when you overcome that challenge. Responsibility does not get developed by walking backward or remaining stuck. Your level of responsibility will be determined by what you do moving forward, starting today!

11. LEARN HOW TO BUILD A STRONG WORK ETHIC WITH ZAIN

" For anyone reading, the Perfect Ten is the embodiment of the mental determination you can find in these featured people. There could be a perfect 100, perfect 1 million, perfect infinity. Anything that is obtainable can be obtainable for you."

— ZAIN

W-inning by
O-utworking
R-ivals,
K-nowing that

E-nthusiasm
T-riumphs and
H-eart
I-nspires
C-hampionships

———

Work ethic is the ultimate equalizer. Whole-hearted effort and consistency can overcome a multitude of challenges, a lack of natural talent, or a plethora of strong competition. Many assume that work ethic is a synonym for working harder, but it is a more complex idea. Work ethic is the ability to work more consistently and more efficiently, taking daily steps towards a goal without complaint or excuse. For Zain, work ethic elevated every portion of his life and opened up every opportunity he could hope for.

Meet Zain

Zain's position in the "Perfect Ten" is unique. While this book challenges the idea of what it means to be a perfect student, Zain closely fits the traditional model of perfection. He seemingly had his life in order at all times and made success look natural. His many achievements were celebrated often, including the placing of his name on a banner in the school's gym. His life was filled with opportunity and positive momentum. The great challenges he faced were simply the challenges he gave himself as his goals grew larger and more ambitious. His story is about the consistent work ethic that was required for him to maintain his success and continue to excel in everything he strived for.

One of four boys raised in a home with Puerto Rican roots, Zain was constantly surrounded by family. His parents were hard-working, loving people from a Jehovah's Witness background. They constantly modeled an incredible work ethic and drive for success. While they did not push their religious beliefs on Zain and his brothers, the strong values they modeled had a big influence on his mindset. Along with his core family, his parents often took in foster children for short periods of time, leading to a full and active household. Working and living alongside these kids helped him to appreciate the life and opportunities he had. Surrounded by support, high expectations, and a humble nature, Zain became accustomed to success. However, he would be allotted no room for error as a disciplined lifestyle would be the only way to accomplish his goals.

Making the Climb

Zain entered high school as a competitor. He could often be spotted in the crowd of high achieving students and at any extracurricular event that provided him with an opportunity to improve. Attributing his attitude to the desire to compete, he stated,

Competition, in academics and sports, is so important to building your mentality. When I was in a classroom, I wanted to finish taking notes first, get the highest test grade, and have the best presentation. Consistency and work ethic went right with it.

He did this with humility and respect, crediting other students for their hard work and celebrating the accomplishments of his friends. However, he was always striving to do more as an individual.

High school also marked the beginning of his athletic career as a wrestler. Being new to the sport, he knew that a learning curve would take place and he embraced it. He competed against any willing wrestler, followed the instructions of his coaches, and engaged in a variety of clubs and extra programs to improve. Just like his school attitude, he would not accept average as a wrestler. He explained, "All my work ethic I contribute to a single quote – I told this to myself all the time. 'If you're not getting better, you're getting worse.'" His work ethic began propelling him to a higher level of success rapidly. He was learning very early to push his limits and give a wholehearted effort to every match, no matter what the odds were.

Balancing a difficult new athletic endeavor with the demanding schedule of intense classes, Zain knew that he would have to kick his work ethic into overdrive. From the first day, he was determined to put his foot on the gas pedal and keep it there. He explained his drive by saying, "I had a high identification of self. It sounds cheesy, but since I was young, I knew that I wanted to be great, which meant that I needed to have a strong work ethic. I wanted to stay motivated no matter what emotions I was feeling." He had decided to stay true to the way he viewed himself. He was a winner and a champion, which meant he would have to work every day to live out that perception of himself.

Weebling, Wobbling, but Never Falling Over

Work ethic comes with a heavy price. It brings with it a long, cumbersome list of things that cannot be done. For Zain, it meant no sleeping in, no missing practices (even the extra ones), no forgetting homework assignments, and absolutely no following his peers. He lived what many describe as the straight and narrow path, because he had a constant understanding of what was at stake and how easily his dreams could vanish. He described his choice to avoid peer pressure, drinking, drug use, or even electronic cigarettes as an important step, stating,

One mistake, one bad party crashed and all your success can be taken away. Staying out of trouble and resisting peer pressure was super important to my success because I didn't give myself the chance to be associated with things that could hinder my success.

He knew what he was missing out on, and it was difficult sometimes to pass on parties and social gatherings. However, it was always worth the sacrifice in his mind when he considered what he was building towards.

While Zain had a solid foundation, it was constantly tested. The social aspect of high school was as challenging for him as it was for anyone else. He explained,

The most difficult thing for sure was choosing my friends wisely and learning what trust is and who I can trust. It sounds almost dramatic, but when choosing friends, I would ask myself if this was a person I

could be able to trust when we are adults. If the answer was yes and I could see them being a positive influence in the future, then I would be happy to be friends with them now.

Taking it further, Zain's participation in sports and clubs forced him to associate with some students with whom he did not feel comfortable. He learned that he could not isolate himself, so he positioned himself as a leader. This allowed him to set the pace and create acceptable boundaries in his social interactions.

A constant focus on growth had Zain on a trailblazing path. While many would describe him as a perfect student-athlete, he did not see himself as a model of perfection. He still had moments where he would goof off in class. He would occasionally sit in the back and relax for a moment. What separated Zain was not that he could be perfect. It was his ability to remain disciplined and to refocus after every moment of leisure. He did not care to be perfect and simply wanted to get better at everything he did, every day.

Executing the Follow Through

The work ethic Zain demonstrated was complemented by a strong sense of planning. He knew what he wanted to accomplish, and he worked those goals into his schedule. The latter years of his schooling were spent taking college courses at a local campus. This move would allow him to design his own school schedule to accommodate his athletic training. The downside to the college dual-enrollment was the rigor and difficulty of the higher-level college courses. While his work load was more demanding, his time was better placed to strive for the huge goals he had set.

With his unshakeable discipline and years of consistent, daily work, Zain was able to earn his status as a state qualifier in wrestling. A thrilling overtime victory displayed the heart and intensity that he showed in every practice. He had reached his biggest goal as an athlete, one that he had worked towards diligently for three years. While many would be satisfied with such a major accomplishment, he used that success to push himself even harder. He explained, "When I was wrestling, I took a step back and appreciated that it was making me a better person." Wrestling was just one thing he was great at, but he wanted to be competitive at everything he did.

His state-qualifying performance guaranteed that he would leave a permanent mark on the school, yet he pushed even harder in his education journey. His perseverance and consistently high effort led to a variety of academic awards and a large list of college choices for him to pick from. Not wanting to be known as "just an athlete," he worked tirelessly to become a well-rounded scholar-athlete. This attitude continues to follow him in his college career, where he has chosen the challenging major of computer engineering. He did not want to peak in high school, so his work ethic has remained steady, allowing him to attack his college-level studies.

Entering Zain Into the Perfect Ten

Many of the "Perfect Ten" students have been overlooked because of the non-traditional ways that their mindset allowed them to succeed. I wanted to introduce Zain because while he would not be overlooked in terms of his levels of success, people still overlooked how hard it was for him to consistently produce at the level he held. Teachers, coaches, parents, and his peers would all look at him as the model of a perfect student, yet few saw how hard he worked to reach that point.

I was privileged to see Zain's journey on a daily basis. For three years, we would spend around three hours per day of training. I would have to stop the practice because he would push himself indefinitely. Yet, he always managed to stay on top of his grades and excel in the classroom throughout the grueling days of practices and the long weekends of competitions.

For students who appear to be perfect, it is a daily struggle for them to not only maintain their levels of success but also to find ways to grow and push themselves beyond their already lofty accomplishments. It can be easy to take a student like Zain for granted, believing that he will wake up each day and carry himself like a champion. Only Zain knew how difficult it was to make that choice every day, resisting temptations to quit, to be lazy for a day, or to make a bad decision for once. His discipline, focus, and incredible work ethic made him an important choice for my "Perfect Ten."

My New Definition of the Perfect Student

The perfect student:

- Hustles harder than their peers because of an unyielding passion that they possess.
- Embraces their identity, honoring and valuing the unique qualities and passions that they possess.
- Has an unyielding mental toughness that pushes them past any barrier or limitation that stands in their way.
- Knows how to remain optimistic and apply it to their everyday lives.
- Is committed to bouncing back and remaining resilient, no matter what happens to them.
- Remains patient and works steadily and consistently towards their goals.
- Shows genuine kindness and seeks to serve others freely.
- Is confident in their ability to learn, progress, and reach new levels.
- Holds themselves responsible and finds a way to complete the tasks they have set out to do.
- **Outworks their peers with perseverance and a focused determination.**

Your New Definition of the Perfect Student

Did this chapter impact your definition of a perfect student? How important does work ethic rank when considering the strengths of a student? Flip back to the introduction and look over your first definition. Reflect on what you said and what you read. Is your definition firm, or is it shifting? Write down your reflections in this space, or continue revising your definition:

Mindset Lesson

Work ethic is a choice, albeit a difficult one, that can be influenced or changed on a daily basis. Discipline and a high level of self-esteem will be your friends as you try to ramp up your work ethic. Zain offered two strong pieces of advice for anyone who wanted a stronger work ethic. First, he suggested, "Stay consistent in everything you do. Pick something and do it every day. If that means perfect attendance at school, that could be it. One pushup a day, that could be it. Consistency builds determination."

While consistent habits were a key in Zain's life, he also offered this second guiding principle: "The foundation of any mental strength that you have begins by remembering to stay human. Everyone is human. Every amazing accomplishment you've heard of was done by a person. Don't think that thing that person did is out of reach for you. They are human, you are human, you could do it too if not better."

Following Zain's advice, here are five ways to improve your work ethic:

1. Develop a consistent routine and hold yourself accountable to stick with it
2. Compete and participate in challenges, no matter how big or small
3. To increase your self-esteem, write down why you deserve to succeed at every goal you set
4. Set boundaries and place your health, happiness, and well-being above short-term pleasures that may set you back farther, like laziness, addictions, or unhealthy habits
5. Choose your friends wisely and contribute meaningfully to the lives of the friends that you do choose

Overlooking the Work Ethic

There exists a thought that the hardest working students have no trouble continuing to hold to their work ethic. It is easy to assume that people like Zain will always give their full effort into every task without complaint or difficulty. Often that assumption is verified because people with strong work ethics rarely complain. However, the assumption can be dangerous for yourself and for how you may overlook others.

Believing that the hard work is easy can minimize the effort that a student has put in, or the challenges they overcame to bring that effort to the classroom. Similarly, it may influence you to think they are just natural hard workers that do not require much effort. It happens surprisingly often. Do not underestimate the strong work ethic of a student. They must make incredible sacrifices to their short term joy and their social life to maintain the level of work they produce. Understanding and compassion can go a long way to encouraging their best work and helping them to balance their life.

Make it Yours

The stronger your work ethic is, the higher your ceiling for success is. You may have noticed in this chapter that Zain was a state qualifier, not a state champion. With all the hard and consistent work he put in, he still suffered losses to incredibly talented wrestlers who were also living a clean and healthy life. However, he surpassed a majority of the state, including many athletes who had many more years of experience on the wrestling mat. If he did not pursue this passion with all of his heart and a consistent effort, he would have had very little chance to reach the highest levels of the state. He managed this while having a fun, light-hearted attitude and a great circle of friends. He explained, "people say you can't have it all, but that's not true, the only one stopping you from obtaining anything you want, is you."

Wherever you are at right now, and whatever your passion is, there is still another level you can reach. Work ethic is the key that unlocks the door of your future success. Where can you become more consistent? What can you make more efficient in your daily process? How can you maximize your potential? Move with intention and utilize a renewed, powerful work ethic to see what happens when you live life to the fullest.

12. THE UNMENTIONED PERFECT STUDENTS

I was honored to be able to take these ten stories and give voice to them in the form of a book. For each of the Perfect Ten students featured here, they decided to be vulnerable and allowed their experiences to be used to make a positive impact on others. I will forever be thankful for the opportunity to hear and understand their stories myself, let alone being given the chance to share them widely with others. Their bravery and honest introspection have led to a set of inspiring stories that are empowering for students around the world.

While the Perfect Ten was packed with incredible students, it is vital to consider the many other amazing students with whom I have had the pleasure of interacting. Teaching has given me the privilege of learning from thousands of students. It would be a large underestimation to think only ten of those thousands had elements of perfection to them. It is quite the opposite. One of the most difficult decisions I had to make in writing this book was determining which ten of my former students should be highlighted. So many young men and women have influenced my view of perfection through the way they utilized their mindset to become successful. This book could have been written in many different ways, featuring an entirely different cast of incredible young leaders.

Should I have included the student who carried a perfect GPA, graduating in three years, who is about to begin her master's degree while also pursuing her love of dance? Would it have been wise for me to include the student who completed zero assignments for most of his high school career until he learned how the school could actually connect to his passion of becoming a professional jeweler, raising his grades almost instantly to graduate and getting into a jewelry trade school? What about the several wonderful students who entered my class in the English for Speakers of Other Languages program and learned the language so well in one year that they all moved into honors English classes in the following year? Is there a place in a book like this for the former drug dealer who was lost in a different world, went into recovery, re-entered school, and successfully graduated while staying clean?

The answer is a resounding yes! All of these students belong in this book. They may not all fit the traditional narrative of perfection, which is a great thing. Their unique successes have become motivational stories that help others to achieve in their own unique ways. Every student I have taught possessed a characteristic, skill, or quality that allowed them to stand out. Yet, those qualities were often silenced or overshadowed by the norms of the typical educational environment. The expectations placed by traditional educators did not match the reality they were facing. Instead of learning and understanding the mindset of these outstanding youth, they shut down the very qualities that made them successful.

A striking realization I had while considering the idea of perfection was the way that my students had been treated in school. Several of my students have gone into the music industry with varying degrees of success. They were remarkably skilled at writing intriguing lyrics with complex patterns. Yet, most of them were in a credit recovery class for English. It did not add up until they explained to me that their skills were devalued by the average adult. They were too vocal in class and full of energy and movement. Often, they complained that they needed to learn out loud and be able to talk about the lesson to understand it. Heavy limits were placed on them due to it not looking like the traditional view of learning that many have. Trouble and bad grades followed their high school careers, regardless of how talented and studious they were.

Elevating Student Voice

The Perfect Ten students deserve to have their voices heard, as do many of my other students. When the narrative of the "model student" does not include their experiences, the world is not ready to promote their strengths and help them overcome their weaknesses. Too often, underestimated young women and men begin to believe that they are not as valuable or worthy as others for success. Those thoughts are based on the assumption that perfection is what it looks like in the media. Reinforced by the stories of adults and people in power across the globe, some characteristics are promoted while others are seen as a hindrance to success.

The perception of perfection can be damaging for many students. They may grow to see their natural talents and strengths as a curse, while their peers become more favored for having strengths that fit the mainstream view of studiousness. The further they drift from their own idea of perfection, the more likely they are to embrace the other and more damaging idea: that they are not good enough. As kids are devalued, they learn to devalue the things that make up their character, leaving them stuck with a low sense of self-esteem and a high amount of stress in trying to adapt to the values that are more commonly praised.

A crucial step in empowering today's youth is the elevation of student voices. For the ten students in this book, they were able to give a realistic view of how their mindset allowed them to succeed on their own terms. Telling their stories validated their journey and the many obstacles they had to overcome to find their way to their goals. Unfortunately, not many students are given the opportunity to share their voice or even hear the voices of other students like them. This leads to kids having misconceptions about success, false ideas of their mindset that may turn a strength into weakness, and an overwhelming sense of being insufficient in the crowd of their peers.

Define Bad

Who are the "bad kids"? This book challenges the idea of perfection because there are millions of young men and women with qualities that go underappreciated and underutilized. To better understand this concept, consider the bad kids. We all know the bad kids. If you are a student, you watch them act out in class and wonder if they will get in trouble again. If you are a teacher, they are the names that get launched around the faculty lounge when other teachers brag about how often they suspended them. If you are a parent, they are the group of kids you absolutely do not want your kid to talk to. Who knows, the bad kid may even be you.

Hopefully, you can see the sarcasm dripping off of the phrase "bad kid" every time I write it. I use the phrase because we often hear it, and most have a clear picture of who it refers to. Take that picture and begin to challenge your assumptions. What makes someone a bad kid? What qualities do they possess that make them difficult, unruly, or incapable of being successful? What stands out about them in terms of their characteristics?

Now imagine what would happen if we took the approach that the Perfect Ten exemplified? If every so-called bad kid was given the opportunity to share their story, what would they say? What strengths would they consider themselves to have? What aspect of their mindset could teach us something about the world and how we live? What barriers exist that prevent them from achieving in the way that they might have hoped for?

The reason that perfect kids and bad kids may look and seem like a stereotype is that they often do not get to share their narrative. A majority of the questions posed here go unanswered. As schools, society, and the world provide a blanket view of the perfect student, the voices of many are covered and stifled. The idea of "perfect students" and the assumptions made of "bad kids" would look drastically different if they all had a platform to share their experiences with the adults of their lives listening attentively.

Listening to students has become the most fulfilling and educational experience of my career. The more time I invested in allowing them to share and teach me, the more powerful my class time would be with them. As they found their voice and realized that many of their "shortcomings" were more about perceptions than reality, the more confidence they built. Redefining perfection happened as a process that we shared together. Along with the Perfect Ten, all of my students have had an amazingly positive influence on me in considering how I view people. I look for strengths instead of harping on weaknesses. I ask instead of tell. I observe instead of imposing. My students have taught me through their triumphs and tragedies alike that they all have meaningful contributions to the world that deserve to be heard, recognized, and acted upon.

13. THE PERFECT ELEVEN

You have met my Perfect Ten. I genuinely hope that you enjoyed their stories and learned from them as I did. Their unbridled passion for improvement motivated me on a daily basis. But it is not about me, and it is not about the Perfect Ten. It is about you.

What do you need to do to become the Perfect Eleven? What would your chapter look like, and how do you want to continue writing it? The stories and experiences included in this book were shared to influence you to action. No matter what stage of life you are in right now, there is another level you can reach. It is my hope and the wish of the Perfect Ten that their shared experiences will assist you in strengthening your mindset and living beyond the potential you currently think you have.

My New Definition of Perfect

Let's revisit my running definition of the perfect student. I hesitate to call it final, because my students continue to reshape and redefine it for me every year.

THE PERFECT STUDENT:

- **Hustles** harder than their peers because of an unyielding passion that they possess.
- Embraces their **identity**, honoring and valuing the unique qualities and passions that they possess.
- Has an unyielding **mental toughness** that pushes them past any barrier or limitation that stands in their way.
- Knows how to remain **optimistic** and apply it to their everyday lives.
- Is committed to bouncing back and remaining **resilient**, no matter what happens to them.
- Remains **patient** and works steadily and consistently towards their goals.
- Shows genuine **kindness** and seeks to serve others freely.
- Is **confident** in their ability to learn, progress, and reach new levels.
- Holds themselves **responsible** and finds a way to complete the tasks they have set out to do.
- **Outworks** their peers with perseverance and a focused determination.

REFLECTING on the Perfect Ten and the many unmentioned students who have had a positive impact on me, there is a theme throughout my definition. Perfect students have a voice. They know this on a deep, internal level, and they fight to bring that voice to the surface. They speak up for themselves and create their own value and self-worth. They use their voice to soak in the positivity of others and equally use their voice to knock down the doubt and negative talk of others.

Are You Perfect?

After reading and reflecting, what is your definition of the perfect student? What values have come to the surface? Is there anything you used to find important in that definition that you have decided to change or drop completely?

I challenge you to write two statements as you finish this book and begin to apply what you've read to your life. First, write your completed new definition of the perfect student. Just like in the beginning, be clear and specific to the best of your ability.

Once you have written your new definition, write down a description of yourself. Begin with the phrase, "I am." Give an honest and open reflection of who you are and how you fit your own definition of perfect. See yourself in your definition and choose to value your own experiences. You belong in this definition and deserve to see what life will be like when you believe in yourself unconditionally. Mark down your thoughts and reflections and use that writing as your official welcome to the Perfect Ten!

Your Definition of the Perfect Student:

I Am:

ABOUT THE AUTHOR

Kevin Leichtman is the co-founder of TLC Educate (http://tlceducate.com), Director of Academic Mindset, and an adjunct professor at Florida Atlantic University. He has taught English and Reading in every grade from 7-12.

Kevin received his M.Ed. and Ph.D. in Curriculum and Instruction from FAU. His dissertation focused on the impact of burnout on new teachers. He has been published in a textbook on Andragogical and Pedagogical methods and was the co-author of the book, "Teacher's Guide to the Mental Edge."

EduMatch Publishing

CPSIA information can be obtained
at www.ICGtesting.com
Printed in the USA
LVHW050525150321
681564LV00017B/1160

9 781953 852120